DEFINITION

boom / ˈbuːm / noun

1:

: a step-by-step manual for resisting authoritarian regimes in the 21st c through peaceful resistance, chutzpah, mischief, and time-tested principles of rebellion

2:

: a loud sound

: an exclamation used to define / draw attention to an excellent outcome, e.g.:

1) to clarify a point
 2) to show respect
 3) to highlight something, or
 4) to indicate suddenness, as an interjection:
 "Then boom, he was fired"
 "I just made the most awesome dinner - boom!"
 "You're such a douche bag - boom!"

3:

: a long spar used to extend the foot of a sail on a boat

4:

: a chain or line of connected floating timbers extended across a river, lake, or harbor to obstruct passage or catch floating objects

Copyright © 2025 by Athena

All rights reserved.

No part of this book may be reproduced in any form or by any electronic or mechanical means, including information storage and retrieval systems, without written permission from the author, except for the use of brief quotations in a book review.

❀ Formatted with Vellum

BOOM

ATHENA

CONTENTS

Preface	vii
1. Hallmarks of an Authoritarian Regime	1
2. Overview of Authoritarian Governments	3
3. The Power of Non-Violence	10
4. Rules for Radicals	20
5. Creating the Infrastructure for Resistance	23
6. Energetic Non-Violence	35
7. Demonstrations	37
8. Seven Ways to Communicate with Authoritarian Supporters	44
9. Comprehensive Plans for Demonstration Safety	47
10. Bystander Intervention	52
11. You and the Law	56
12. Resilience and Repair	61
13. Creative Resistance: A Short History of Creative Acts of Rebellion	70
14. Using Psychological Tactics Against the Regime	77
15. Disrupt the Regime's Supply Chain	80
16. Narrative Warfare	89
17. Spreading Information Without Getting Caught	93
18. Using Artificial Intelligence Tools	97
19. Cyber Resistance Methods	102
20. Drones: An Evolving Tool for Activism	110
21. Applying Sun Tzu's The Art of War to 21st Century Resistance	114
22. Mischief	127
23. Reading List	132
About the Author	135

PREFACE

Welcome to *Boom: The Manual for Nonviolent Insurrection In The 21st Century*.

This small blue book offers practical steps for mounting peaceful, active rebellions against authoritarian regimes in the 21st c., using contemporary activist tools along with the time-tested principles of Sun Tzu.

You are reading this book because you want things to change: you are concerned about your country, your fellow citizens, and want the world to be a better place.

First, we provide a broad overview of the characteristics, policies, and initiatives of authoritarian regimes, with brief introductions to resistance methods.

Second, you will find detailed programs for resistance, coupled with descriptions of what has worked and not worked in the historical record of working for freedom and dignity versus authoritarian regimes.

It was written specifically in response to the policies and practices of a new administration in Washington, DC, USA, in early 2025, but the principles of this book can be applied widely.

It does not promote sedition or insurrection nor give

instructions on how to carry out illegal activities. Rather, it offers publicly-available tools, resources, and ideas for those in need, a clearinghouse of information to be updated regularly online.

Although the American executive administration of early 2025 cannot yet be compared to historically authoritarian or totalitarian regimes, it has been labelled "fascist" by many commentators due to its alliance with extreme right causes and politicians, and its dramatic and possibly illegal activities.

As of April 2025, there have already been many mass demonstrations and other actions in opposition to the Trump Administration.

Please note that there are many activist groups already in existence, and so it is not necessary to re-invent the wheel. Please do a thorough search and align yourself with existing groups, unless your principles and goals are best met by working separately.

There are also many issues on which to focus when resisting an authoritarian regime, from environmental subjects, to health care, to legal topics.

Don't try to take them all on yourself: you will burn out and become overwhelmed. Instead, pick an area that is close to your heart and align yourself with others who feel similarly.

There are many ways to be involved in resistance movements, from quiet back-room research and fundraising, to walking in the streets, shouting slogans and carrying posters.

Our guides have been Buddhist ethical principles as well as Western principles embodied in things as common as 12 Step Programs. *"Principles above personalities"* is a 12 Step tradition that means placing common principles (ethics, guidelines, steps) above your own ego or the ego of others.

A principled resistance movement attempts to act through ethical guidelines that include not harming other people directly, but it does not exclude direct actions that may interfere with the functioning of authoritarian institutions, infrastructure, or "human capital."

There are many resistance efforts in the past that have succeeded in changing regimes and policies, but mention of these will be brief: you can look them up for more details.

Similarly, specific directions for violent resistance methods are not included, since you can find such information on your own. Searching for "how to create an incendiary device with household items" on TOR will give you results, in other words (TOR = "The Onion Router," a safe browser to use in order to avoid detection while searching the internet).

When doing searches, be sure to use a browser such as TOR, and/or use a VPN, in order to attempt to maintain privacy and to be able to search more deeply and with less outside surveillance.

Some starting principles of effective resistance:

- Change must come from principles.
- Every action you take should be guided by principles by which you attempt to abide.
- You are not just fighting *against* a regime; you are also fighting FOR something in which you believe.
- Begin with chutzpah, and end with wisdom and care.
- Common welfare comes first: this includes the welfare of others who might disagree with you.
- "Begin with the end in mind," (Stephen Covey, *7 Habits of Highly Effective People*)
- Know your enemy's vulnerabilities, and your own.
- Work with trusted partners.
- Live to fight another day.
- All's fair in love and war.
- Be peaceful, powerful, sneaky, mischievous, and kind.

- Use your anger wisely: be fed by it, but do not let it rule you.
- Use your opponent's energy against them like an aikido master: if they move in to strike, pull them towards you and encourage them to fall.
- Have fun.
- When in doubt, don't.
- Toss flowers to onlookers at a demonstration (instead of bricks).

CHAPTER 1
HALLMARKS OF AN AUTHORITARIAN REGIME

The Authoritarian Regime's Agenda

- Win elections on fear & populist promises
- Reclaim power for the People from the "elites"
- Purge highest positions in key government institutions
- Place cronies in positions of highest power regardless of their competence
- Brush off any critical press as "fake," "corrupt," and "acting against the People"
- Bluntly lie to the People
- Ban press from parliament/congress/White House or selectively limit their access
- Limit press freedom & quietly take control of mainstream media
- Label opposition & protesters as "traitors," or "elites trying to reclaim power"
- Limit freedom of assembly
- Fix highest court to be able to bypass Constitution, "for the good of the people"
- Limit minority & women's rights

- Ruin the economy to fulfill populist promises in the short term
- Alienate international partners and allies, "making the country great again"
- Quietly fix electoral law under the disguise of making it better
- Start over, until there's nothing left…

(From Eastern European Twitter postings in 2017)

CHAPTER 2
OVERVIEW OF AUTHORITARIAN GOVERNMENTS

CENTRALIZATION OF POWER

- Power is concentrated in the hands of a single leader (e.g., a dictator), a small group of elites, or a specific political party.
- This often undermines or completely bypasses democratic institutions like the judiciary, legislature, or electoral system.
- Decision-making is often opaque, and the leader or ruling party operates without the checks and balances present in democratic systems, or ignores them.

LACK OF POLITICAL PLURALISM

- Political opposition is suppressed, and there is little or no freedom of political expression.
- Political parties or movements that challenge the ruling authority are often banned, co-opted, heavily controlled, or actively discredited, often falsely.

- Authoritarian governments often invoke emergency powers or declare martial law. These powers typically allow the regime to:
  - suspend constitutional rights,
  - imprison dissenters without trial, and
  - take control of the economy and other institutions.
- Authoritarian governments pass new laws or amend constitutions to ensure the power remains in the hands of the leader. This can include
  - provisions for indefinite terms in office,
  - elimination of term limits, or
  - weakening the legislature and judiciary.

Limited Civil Liberties

- Civil rights such as freedom of speech, freedom of assembly, freedom of the press, and the right to a fair trial are significantly restricted or abolished.
- Citizens are not able to express dissent without facing consequences.
- Authoritarian governments often take control of the media, either through direct ownership of news outlets or through censorship, and use it to disseminate propaganda and suppress any critical coverage of the government.
- Dissenting journalists may be jailed, silenced, or forced to conform to state narratives.
- Authoritarian governments attempt to control the internet, by
  - blocking access to foreign news sources,
  - limiting social media platforms, or
  - surveilling online activity to track and suppress dissent.

Rule by Law, Not Rule of Law

- In authoritarian regimes, laws are typically used as a tool for maintaining the power of the regime rather than protecting individual rights or ensuring justice.
- Legal systems are manipulated to serve the needs of the ruling authority.
- The judiciary may be politicized or controlled by the government to ensure that laws are applied in a way that benefits the regime.

Control Over Military, Security, and Paramilitary Forces

- Authoritarian regimes maintain tight control over the military, police, and intelligence services to prevent dissent from within the armed forces.
- Loyalty from the military and police may be ensured in exchange for power or benefits.
- Many authoritarian regimes use paramilitary groups, secret police, or surveillance networks to monitor and control the population.
- These groups are often given broad powers to arrest, torture, and kill without due process.
- Some groups may not be officially connected to the regime, but are tacitly approved by the regime, such as various right-wing groups in the USA in 2025 like the "J6" people who were pardoned by their ally President Trump.

Manipulation or Disregard of Elections

- If elections are held, they are typically rigged,

manipulated, or controlled in such a way that the ruling party or leader is guaranteed to win.
- Voter suppression, vote tampering, or disqualifying opposition candidates are common tactics.
- In some cases, elections may be held in name only, with the outcome predetermined or highly constrained.

Suppression of Dissent

- Any form of protest, whether by individuals or organized groups, is often met with violent repression or legal consequences.
- Human rights organizations, activists, and journalists critical of the regime may be harassed, imprisoned, or silenced.
- Surveillance of citizens is often implemented as a tool of control in authoritarian regimes.
    - This can include monitoring phone calls, emails, social media activity, and even employing facial recognition technology.
- In some authoritarian regimes, governments encourage or incentivize citizens to inform on each other, creating a climate of fear and suspicion where trust among the population is undermined.
- Fear is broadly used as a tactic: ranging from fear of being fired from a job to fear of oneself or one's family being exiled or killed.
    - Consider American citizens who may be afraid to speak out in the early 2025 social climate, where many have been fired from federal positions.

"Legalized" Discrimination

- State-sanctioned discrimination: authoritarian governments may enact laws that favor a particular ethnic, religious, or social group while marginalizing others.
    - These laws could include restrictions on voting rights, education, employment, and free movement.
- They may use existing laws and twist them, rewording their intention to suit their own needs and agenda.
- Segregation and social division: policies that encourage social division, along ethnic, racial, or religious lines, are often used by authoritarian regimes to create a "divide and conquer" situation.
- By sowing division among the populace, the regime can prevent the rise of a unified opposition.

Control of the Economy

- State control of key industries like energy, transportation, and defense, using them to consolidate power and enrich loyalists.
- Economic policies that reward supporters of the regime while punishing or ignoring dissidents.
    - This includes manipulating subsidies, tariffs, and other trade regulations to benefit certain groups, companies, or regions.
- The regime rewards loyalty with wealth, power, and state contracts, creating a system of crony capitalism.
- When elites benefit financially from supporting the regime, it fosters an environment of corruption.

- Wealth is concentrated among a small group of people, leading to inequality and the undermining of institutions that should serve the public good.
  - Corruption also reduces the state's ability to provide essential services like education, healthcare, and infrastructure.
- Regimes often create systems of patronage, where loyalty is rewarded with government contracts, land, or resources.
  - This incentivizes those in power to perpetuate the regime and suppress any attempts at reform.
- Authoritarian regimes often gain financial backing from foreign governments or multinational corporations, especially if those entities have vested interests in the regime's survival. In turn, the regime ensures access to resources or markets that benefit these foreign partners.

Suppression of Education

- Education systems under authoritarian regimes are heavily censored to prevent the spread of ideas that could challenge the authority of the regime.
- History is rewritten to highlight the legitimacy of the ruling government and to suppress any opposing narratives.
- Higher education institutions are often targeted, as universities can be hotbeds of dissent and critical thinking. Faculty members may be purged if they are suspected of harboring dissenting views.
- Research in the social sciences, humanities, or any field that challenges the regime's narrative is heavily controlled.

Suppression of the Arts

- The arts are often subjected to strict state control to prevent works that could challenge the regime's power or promote alternative ideologies.
- Writers, musicians, filmmakers, and other artists are often watched by the state. Artists who engage in subversive activities, such as producing underground works or participating in dissident movements, may be imprisoned, tortured, or exiled.

"The outstanding negative quality of the totalitarian elite is that it never stops to think about the world as it really is and never compares the lies with reality."
— Hannah Arendt

Before mass leaders seize the power to fit reality to their lies, their propaganda is marked by its extreme contempt for facts as such, for in their opinion fact depends entirely on the power of man who can fabricate it.
— Hannah Arendt

CHAPTER 3
THE POWER OF NON-VIOLENCE

F*irst, they ignore you, then they ridicule you, then they fight you, and then you win.* - Gandhi, *The Philosophy of Non-Violence*

Non-violence is rooted in the belief that it is better to resist injustice without causing harm to others. This philosophy can be traced back to the teachings of figures like Mahatma Gandhi, who used it as a foundation for India's struggle for independence, and Dr. Martin Luther King Jr., who led the Civil Rights Movement in the United States.

Non-violence is not a passive response; it is an active form of resistance that requires immense courage, coordination, and strategy.

Key Strengths of Non-Violent Resistance

By refusing to use force, the movement prevents the regime from framing the opposition as "terrorists" or "criminals." This, in turn, helps to maintain international support and sympathy for the cause.

- Non-violent movements attract not only those who are directly oppressed but also those who feel empathy for the cause.
- This broadens the base of support and helps to create a sense of solidarity among disparate groups.
- It also attracts attention from the international community, which can put additional pressure on the regime.
- Non-violence works by disrupting the existing systems of power, often through methods such as boycotts, strikes, and mass protests.
- These disruptions cause enough chaos to weaken the regime's hold over the people and its control of economic and political systems, without the use of physical violence.

Why Non-Violent Resistance Works

While authoritarian regimes may have the military power to crush violent uprisings, they are often far less capable of quelling large-scale, non-violent movements.

This is because non-violent resistance doesn't rely on combat, which is easy for authoritarian forces to suppress with military force; instead, *it challenges the very legitimacy of the regime.*

Several factors contribute to the success of non-violent resistance:

- Wide participation: non-violence allows for a greater number of people to participate in the movement, including those who might fear the risks associated with violent confrontation.
- This means that more people can become involved, creating a larger, more diverse base of support.
  - Elderly people, people with disabilities, and even children can participate in marches, letter-

writing, and demonstrations, illustrating to the regime and to the world the wide-spread nature of resistance.
- Undermining legitimacy: if the regime resorts to violence against peaceful demonstrators, it risks losing both domestic and international support.
- Economic pressure: non-violent resistance often includes economic boycotts, work stoppages, and civil disobedience that disrupt the economy.
    - The longer the resistance persists, the more pressure it places on the regime's ability to maintain control.

Non-Violent Tactics and Strategies

- **Civil disobedience**: refusing to obey unjust laws or orders can have a profound impact.
    - Acts of civil disobedience—such as refusing to pay taxes, engaging in sit-ins, or occupying government buildings—disrupt the functioning of the regime and draw attention to the injustice being fought.
- **Boycotts and strikes**: economic disruptions, such as boycotts of government-owned businesses, strikes by workers, and halting production in key industries, can cripple an authoritarian regime's ability to operate.
- **Non-violent protest and demonstrations**: mass protests and demonstrations can mobilize large portions of the population, creating a powerful visual message of defiance. When done peacefully, these protests are more difficult to justify military repression against, especially in the eyes of international observers.

- **Mass non-cooperation**: encouraging individuals to withdraw their support from the regime—whether by refusing to participate in government-sponsored activities or by simply refusing to collaborate—can destabilize the system and create a domino effect.
- **Information and media campaigns**: the dissemination of information—through pamphlets, underground media, social media platforms, and more—can help expose the truth, raise awareness, and counter the regime's propaganda.
    - This is especially important in the age of digital manipulation, where regimes often use media to control narratives.

Non-Violent Success Stories

- *Gandhi's Salt March* (1930): In colonial India, Mahatma Gandhi led a non-violent campaign against British rule. The Salt March was a key example of civil disobedience, where Gandhi and his followers marched to the sea to make salt in defiance of British laws. The movement galvanized millions, leading to India's independence from British colonial rule in 1947.
- The *Civil Rights Movement* (1950s-1960s): In the United States, the Civil Rights Movement, led by figures like Dr. Martin Luther King Jr., used non-violent methods such as sit-ins, protests, and marches to challenge segregation and racism. The movement ultimately led to the passage of key civil rights legislation, including the Civil Rights Act of 1964 and the Voting Rights Act of 1965.
- The *Solidarity Movement* in Poland (1980s): In Poland, the Solidarity trade union movement led by

Lech Wałęsa used strikes and non-violent resistance to challenge the communist regime. Despite government repression, the movement grew to become a powerful force that played a key role in ending communist rule in Poland and inspiring similar movements across Eastern Europe.

- The *Arab Spring* (2010-2012): While not all outcomes of the Arab Spring were successful, the movement showed the power of non-violent resistance in the face of repressive regimes. In countries like Tunisia and Egypt, mass protests and civil disobedience led to the ousting of long-standing dictators, even though violent suppression by the regimes was common.

"Between 1900 and 2006, nonviolent resistance campaigns were nearly twice as likely to achieve full or partial success as their violent counterparts." - Erica Chenoweth, Maria J. Stephan, *Why Civil Resistance Works: The Strategic Logic of Nonviolent Conflict*

Gandhi Salt March, India

Checklist for Building a Foundation for Resistance

- Create a unified movement:
  - Ensure that people from various backgrounds and ideologies can come together for a common cause, inclusive and representative of diverse communities.
- Define a common vision for the present and the future:
  - It is essential to address key issues such as social justice, political freedom, economic equality, and human rights.
  - A vision that speaks to these concerns can attract widespread support.
- Build a broad coalition: include not only those directly affected by the authoritarian regime but also those who can lend political, economic, and intellectual support. This may include:
  - labor unions,
  - human rights organizations,
  - community groups,
  - academics, and
  - international allies.
- Community engagement:
  - neighborhood meetings,
  - local protests, or
  - efforts to provide services in areas the regime neglects.
- Spread the message: develop a clear and compelling message that resonates with the public.
  - The message should focus on the values that the movement is fighting for—freedom, justice, and equality—and emphasize the importance of non-violent resistance.

- Social media platforms and traditional forms of communication, like leaflets and posters, can be instrumental in spreading the message.
- Train and empower citizens:
    - Workshops on non-violent methods of resistance,
    - Self-defense, and
    - Digital security

Leadership in Non-Violent Resistance

Non-violent movements require a leadership style that is strategic, ethical, and capable of maintaining morale in the face of repression.

Non-violent resistance movements need leaders who can inspire others through words, actions, and commitment to the cause.

- Decentralized leadership:
    - While a strong leader can play an important role, it's essential that a non-violent movement avoids becoming overly reliant on a single individual.
    - Principles over personalities.
    - One of the strengths of non-violence is that it is difficult to disrupt through targeted attacks on leaders.
    - A decentralized structure allows the movement to maintain flexibility and resilience, even if certain leaders are targeted or arrested.
- Train leaders at all levels:
    - To ensure the movement's continuity, leadership must be cultivated at all levels.

- This involves training local organizers, community leaders, and activists in strategic thinking, public speaking, and non-violent tactics.
  - A well-trained leadership core helps ensure that the movement stays focused and that decisions can be made quickly in times of crisis.
- Role of symbolic leaders:
  - In addition to practical leaders who manage the day-to-day operations, symbolic leaders can help rally the masses and maintain the movement's moral authority.
  - These individuals often embody the movement's values and ideals, and their actions can inspire people to continue participating in the struggle for change.

Set Clear and Achievable Goals

Every revolutionary movement must have clear, actionable objectives that can be pursued step-by-step.

Short-term goals might include:

- organizing protests,
- engaging in acts of civil disobedience,
- or gaining media attention.

Long-term goals involve more significant political and societal changes, such as the removal of the authoritarian regime and the establishment of a new political system.

Measurable milestones: For the movement to stay motivated, it is crucial to set measurable milestones. Examples of milestones could be:

- a specific number of people joining the movement,
- a successful boycott, or

- the resignation of key government officials.

Understand the Regime's Vulnerabilities

An essential part of goal-setting is to understand where the regime is most vulnerable.

Whether it's economic instability, political divisions, or weakened military morale, identifying these vulnerabilities allows the movement to craft strategies that target the regime's weakest points.

Goals should be aligned with these vulnerabilities, so that each action helps to weaken the regime and pave the way for further resistance.

Summary of Key Nonviolent Strategies
Civil disobedience

- The deliberate and public violation of laws or regulations that are considered unjust,
- That challenge the legitimacy of the regime, and
- Disrupt the normal functioning of society, making it difficult for the authoritarian regime to maintain control without exposing its oppressive nature

Strikes and boycotts

- Target key industries: identify industries or sectors that are crucial to the regime's economic power (e.g., oil, transportation, telecommunications) and target them with strikes or work stoppages.
- Coordinate action: strikes are most effective when they involve a wide range of sectors, from industrial workers to office employees.

Coordination is key to creating a critical mass that cannot be ignored.

Sit-ins and occupations

- Strategic locations: occupy symbolic locations, such as government buildings, transport hubs, or economic centers, that disrupt the regime's ability to function normally.
- Remain peaceful and determined.

Non-Cooperation

Deliberately refuse to participate in the activities or systems that support the regime. This can include:

- Refusing to pay taxes,
- Not participating in government elections, or
- Refusing to work in state-run institutions,
- Building alternative institutions:
  - parallel economies,
  - independent media outlets and new social media platforms, or
  - local governance structures that challenge the regime's monopoly on power.

Build Institutions

One of the most enduring ways to address authoritarianism is to build or revise the democratic institutions that can sustain a more open, accountable government. This is a long-term effort.

Remember that you are resisting a regime because you want to create a better one, so begin with the end in mind, and work from principles you hold dear.

CHAPTER 4
RULES FOR RADICALS

In 1971, Saul Alinsky wrote an entertaining classic on grassroots organizing titled *Rules for Radicals*. It provides some of the best advice on confrontational tactics.

Alinsky begins this way:

What follows is for those who want to change the world from what it is to what they believe it should be. ***The Prince*** *was written by Machiavelli for the Haves on how to hold power.* ***Rules for Radicals*** *is written for the Have-Nots on how to take it away.*

Alinsky provides a collection of rules to guide the process. But he emphasizes these rules must be translated into real-life tactics that are fluid and responsive to the situation at hand.

Rule 1: Power is not only what you have, but what an opponent thinks you have. If your organization is small, hide your numbers in the dark and raise a din that will make everyone think you have many more people than you do.

Rule 2: Never go outside the experience of your people. The result is confusion, fear, and retreat.

Rule 3: Whenever possible, go outside the experience of an opponent. *Cause* confusion, fear, and retreat.

Rule 4: Make opponents live up to their own book of rules.

Rule 5: Ridicule is man's most potent weapon. It's hard to counterattack ridicule, and it infuriates the opposition, which then reacts to your advantage.

Rule 6: A good tactic is one your people enjoy. "If your people aren't having a ball doing it, there is something very wrong with the tactic."

Rule 7: A tactic that drags on for too long becomes a drag. Commitment may become ritualistic as people turn to other issues.

Rule 8: Keep the pressure on. Use different tactics and actions and use all events of the period for your purpose.

Rule 9: The threat is more terrifying than the thing itself.

When Alinsky leaked word that large numbers of poor people were going to tie up the washrooms of O'Hare Airport, Chicago city authorities quickly agreed to act on a longstanding commitment to a ghetto organization. They imagined the mayhem as thousands of passengers poured off airplanes to discover every washroom occupied. Then they imagined the international embarrassment and the damage to the city's reputation.

Rule 10: The price of a successful attack is a constructive alternative. Avoid being trapped by an opponent or an interviewer who says, "Okay, what would you do?"

Rule 11: Pick the target, freeze it, personalize it, polarize it. Don't try to attack abstract corporations or bureaucracies. *Identify a responsible individual.* Ignore attempts to shift or spread the blame.

According to Alinsky, the main job of the organizer is to bait an opponent into reacting.

"The enemy properly goaded and guided in his reaction will be your major strength."

The major premise for tactics is the development of operations that will maintain a constant pressure upon the opposition. It is this that will cause the opposition to react to your advantage. - Alinsky

Source: https://citizenshandbook.org/rules.html

CHAPTER 5
CREATING THE INFRASTRUCTURE FOR RESISTANCE

*F*UNDRAISING, *C*OMMUNICATION, *I*NTERNET *S*ECURITY, AND *C*ELLS

*F*UNDRAISING *B*ASICS

Every movement needs money – your own or the funds you can raise. If you've been good at raising money in the past, use your skills to help raise money for activism.

Remember, in any fundraising work, you should be as specific as possible in stating your needs for funds and proposing your ideas to potential funders.

While it's easy to propose "We need money to fund travel to demonstrations," it's better to include details that summarize the problems, goals, methods, and expected outcomes of the demonstration, to break down how the funds will be used (personnel costs, equipment, supplies, travel, etc.), and to provide an overview of your organization and its mission.

*C*ROWDFUNDING FOR *R*ESISTANCE *M*OVEMENTS

Crowdfunding has become a significant tool for raising financial support for social and political causes, including resistance movements.

The Hong Kong Protests (2019-2020), The 2011 Egyptian Revolution, and The Syrian Civil War (2011-2024) all used some aspect of crowdfunding to support their causes.

Choose platforms that provide security, anonymity, and flexibility in how funds are managed and distributed.

It's crucial to have someone on your team who is skilled at using these online platforms, especially when BitCoin is involved.

It's also advisable to designate one or more people whose sole function is to raise funds, people who are willing to spend lots of time fine-tuning your appeal and managing the various platforms needed to raise and acquire funds; and people who may be able to source funds directly from wealthy people sympathetic to your cause.

- **GoFundMe** is one of the largest and most popular crowdfunding platforms. It is widely used for personal, charity, and activism campaigns, but does not offer anonymity unless you include Bitcoin processing.
- **Kickstarter**, while not specifically designed for political movements, it can be used to raise money for the production of resistance materials (e.g., books, documentaries, art projects).
- **Indiegogo** is a platform for raising funds for a variety of projects.
- **Patreon** allows creators and activists to receive ongoing financial support from patrons. This model is particularly effective for long-term resistance movements that need continuous financial resources for their operations.
- **GoGetFunding** is a smaller crowdfunding platform that offers flexible funding options and offers a degree of anonymity and international support. It's

used by many grassroots movements for political causes and humanitarian aid.
- **Cryptocurrency Crowdfunding** platforms allow for more anonymity and security than traditional crowdfunding platforms. These include:
    - **BitGive**, which allows donors to contribute without revealing personal information.
    - **BitPatron**: similar to Patreon, BitPatron allows creators to raise funds while accepting cryptocurrency, ensuring greater privacy for both the fundraiser and donors.
    - **GoFundMe (with Bitcoin):** If you want to use a larger platform like GoFundMe, you can still maintain some level of anonymity by funneling donations through Bitcoin, using intermediaries (e.g., wallets), or relying on tools like Bitcoin Payment Processors that integrate with crowdfunding platforms.
    - **Open Collective:** Allows for transparent crowdfunding, but unlike traditional platforms, it focuses on open-source projects and collaborative efforts. It might be a better option for a collective resistance movement that needs transparency with donors while maintaining privacy for those involved.
    - **Decentralized Crowdfunding:** If you need to stay entirely off the grid or avoid platform surveillance, decentralized crowdfunding platforms built on blockchain technology (such as DAO (Decentralized Autonomous Organizations)) can also be used.

The Fundraising Security Checklist

- Create anonymous campaigns: use pseudonyms, encrypted emails, and non-personal information when setting up your campaign.
- Cryptocurrency payments: set up a cryptocurrency wallet to receive donations, and use privacy-focused coins like **Monero** to ensure donor anonymity.
- VPN and Tor: always use a VPN to mask your IP address, and use Tor for browsing the internet or managing campaigns. **ExpressVPN, NordVPN**, and **ProtonVPN** are popular choices.
- Distribute funds securely: use anonymous wallets, prepaid cards, or secure methods of transferring funds to avoid detection.
- Be aware of tracking: avoid using personal email addresses, phone numbers, or IP addresses that could link you to the campaign.
- Set Up Two-Factor Authentication (2FA): add 2FA to all accounts used for organizing the crowdfunding to prevent unauthorized access.
- Collaborate with trusted allies: Build trust among those managing the funds to ensure accountability and prevent infiltration.
- Avoid direct bank transfers: traditional financial systems can be tracked. Whenever possible, opt for anonymous payment methods, such as cryptocurrencies, which offer a layer of privacy.
- Email: set up a secure, anonymous email account. Use services like **ProtonMail** or **Tutanota**, which offer end-to-end encryption. Make sure that this email account is not tied to your personal information or identity.

- Use cryptocurrency for donations: Bitcoin, Ethereum, or Privacy Coins
- Set up a Bitcoin wallet (e.g., Coinbase, Blockchain.info, Electrum, or Monero for privacy) to accept donations.
- Share the wallet address on the crowdfunding platform for people to send donations.
- Use CoinJoin or Mixing Services to anonymize transactions once the funds are received, making it harder to trace the movement of money.
- Stealth donations: allow donors to contribute through anonymous digital wallets.
  - Make sure not to collect any identifying information from donors when using cryptocurrencies.

Communication, Technology and Security

Use tools like Virtual Private Networks (VPNs), encrypted messaging apps (e.g., Signal, Telegram), and the Tor browser to access blocked websites, communicate securely, and share information with the world.

- Use PGP encryption for emails and sensitive files.
- Analog communication: use analog devices, such as short-wave radios and walkie-talkies.
- Use social media cautiously—being aware of surveillance, using aliases, and encrypting sensitive messages.
- Memes, videos, and other visual content can have an outsized influence. Memes are highly shareable, easy to create, and often bypass censorship filters.
- Radio and TV broadcasts: In many countries, underground radio stations or independent media outlets can serve as critical lifelines for spreading news and information.

- Print media and pamphlets: pamphlets, leaflets, posters, stickers, and newspapers can be distributed clandestinely to get the message to a wide audience. These materials can contain key facts, education, inspirational messages, and calls to action.
- Build a network of couriers: in situations where digital and traditional media are unavailable or compromised, underground networks of couriers can be used to disseminate information.

Internet Security Guidelines

The digital age has led to an age of smart repression. My sense is that regimes have basically caught up to whatever advantage there was to the Internet for activists. The Internet provides lots of opportunity for more narrow, discriminating repression that's more effective than the blunt, brute force that would take place in the streets. What happens with social media in particular is that we essentially reveal all of our preferences and activities, publicly or privately, and all those preferences can be very easily surveilled now. Even if you're not saying much, it's not hard to figure out whose side you're on. – Erica Chenoweth, in **Politics of Terror**

GPS—Here we go again, there were 20,189 devices. Still a large crowd but not even close to the 30,000 quoted in Denver newspapers nor the 34,000 quoted by Bernie Sanders and AOC. 84% of the devices present had attended 9 or more Kamala Harris rallies, antifa/blm, pro-Hamas, pro-Palestinian protests, 31% had attended over 20. 90% of those in the above 84% were likely working with one of these five groups and is the reason for their presence. Once again, this is based a very sophisticated algorithm that looks at the behavioral metrics for each device, including the physical 1:1 proximity to leaders and paymasters from these groups in the past. Disruption Project, Rise & Resist, Indivisible Project, Trouble-

makers and the Democratic Socialists of America. we also look at in addition to GPS location data demographic and psychographic data using over 6,000 different databases, i.e., like the Bureau of Labor Statistics (BLS), Pew Research Center, market research firms like YouGov, Experian, specialized tools like ESRI's Tapestry Segmentation, consumer surveys, social media platforms like X, Facebook, LinkedIn. – Tony Sevruga, monitoring a March 2025 demonstration in Denver, CO, via his politically conservative data collection service, quoted on X, March 2025.

The internet is complicated, and so it is crucial to have at least one person on your team who is at home with all of the following information and anti-surveillance methods and can set them up for you. We repeat this information often in this book.

Use a Secure and Anonymous Operating System

- Tails OS: a live operating system that runs from a USB and routes all connections through Tor.
- Whonix: an OS designed for strong anonymity by forcing all internet traffic through Tor.
- Qubes OS: a security-focused OS that isolates different activities into separate virtual machines.

Encrypt Your Internet Traffic

- Use a VPN: A good VPN encrypts your traffic and hides your IP address. Do not use free VPNs.
- Tor Browser: routes traffic through multiple encrypted relays, making it difficult to trace.
- I2P or Freenet: Alternative anonymity-focused networks.

Harden Your Browser and Internet Activity

- Disable JavaScript: JavaScript can be used to fingerprint and track you.
- Use Privacy-Focused Browsers:
  - Brave (with fingerprinting protection)
  - Firefox (hardened with privacy settings and extensions)
  - LibreWolf (a hardened fork of Firefox)
- Extensions to Use:
  - uBlock Origin (ad and tracker blocker
  - NoScript (blocks JavaScript)
  - Privacy Badger (tracker blocker)
  - Cookie AutoDelete (deletes cookies after browsing)

Avoid Logging into Accounts

- Google, Facebook, or other logged-in services tie your activities to your real identity.

Hide Your Identity and Location

- Use disposable identities: avoid using real names, phone numbers, or addresses.
- Use Cryptocurrency (Monero): Monero is a privacy-focused cryptocurrency that is harder to trace than Bitcoin.
- Avoid WiFi networks you don't control: public WiFi can be monitored; use a VPN if you must connect.

Minimize Digital Footprints

- Use virtual machines (VMs): run different activities in separate virtual machines.

- Use burner phones and numbers for online registrations and two-factor authentication.
- Disable location services on all devices.

Advanced Tactics

- Use a Faraday bag to block signals from mobile devices. A Faraday bag has a metallic lining (often a layered fabric of materials like copper, aluminum, or static dissipative polyester) that shields against electromagnetic fields. Faraday bags can block a variety of signals, including cell phone signals, Wi-Fi, Bluetooth, GPS, RFID, and other electromagnetic radiation.
- Randomize MAC addresses to prevent WiFi tracking.
- Avoid using smart devices like smart watches, Amazon's Echo, or smart appliances, which can track your location and listen to you too
- Use offline maps & navigation instead of GPS-dependent apps.

Dealing with Regime Surveillance: Cells

One way to mitigate the risk of surveillance is to organize in a decentralized manner.

Instead of relying on a single leader or centralized structure, movements can divide their efforts into smaller, autonomous groups, or cells.

These groups can operate independently of one another, making it more difficult for the regime to infiltrate or dismantle the movement as a whole.

Cells were active during the American Revolution, the French Resistance in World War Two, and many other situations.

Structure of a Cell-Based Movement

A resistance movement using cells can be structured in two primary ways:

Compartmentalized Hierarchical Cells

- Leadership sets the strategy but does not directly interact with operatives.
- Cells operate in small, independent units (3-7 members) with minimal knowledge of other cells.
- Communication is one-directional to limit exposure.

Networked Cells (Leaderless Resistance)

- Each cell operates autonomously with a common mission but without centralized control. This model is harder to dismantle but requires ideological unity.

Setting Up a cell

- Recruit trusted individuals with verifiable backgrounds.
- New recruits should undergo ideological, psychological, and loyalty testing.
- Individuals should only know their own cell members, not others.
- Keep cells small (3-7 people) to limit exposure.
- Provide specialized training in:
  - Operational Security (OPSEC) – Secure communication, counter-surveillance.
  - Tactics & Strategy – Guerilla tactics, digital resistance, disinformation, civil disobedience.
- Assign specific functions

- Leader/Coordinator – Sets objectives for the cell
- Intelligence Operative – Gathers and relays information
- Logistics Specialist – Manages supplies, safe houses, transportation
- Operations/Action Specialist – Executes tasks (sabotage, dissemination, activism).

COMMUNICATION PROTOCOLS

- Compartmentalization:
  - A cell only communicates with one higher-up, not other cells.
- Dead drops & coded messages:
  - Use physical dead drops, encrypted messages, or anonymous online forums.
- Plausible deniability:
  - If caught, members should only be aware of limited information.
- No electronic footprint:
  - Use secure, disposable communication methods such as analog radio and burner phones.

MANAGING RESOURCES AND LOGISTICS

- Funding: diversify sources—crowdfunding, front businesses, external supporters.
- Safe Houses: establish locations for meetings, training, and escape.

ACTION & COORDINATION

- Mission-based operations:
  - Each cell should have a specific purpose (propaganda, intelligence, direct action).

- Testing before action:
    - Conduct small, low-risk operations to assess effectiveness.
- Backup & contingency plans:
    - Have escape routes, alternative meeting points, and emergency contacts.

Security

- Detect infiltration: regularly check for suspicious behavior among members.
- Code words & false information: occasionally plant false information to test for leaks.
- Rotation of members: change roles or locations periodically to avoid patterns.

———

Please note that the above information was current as of April, 2025, and since internet security is a rapidly evolving area, there could be new information available when you are reading this.

CHAPTER 6
ENERGETIC NON-VIOLENCE

While the goal of non-violent resistance is to minimize harm, there are instances where direct non-lethal actions may be used strategically. These actions should be considered with caution, as they can carry significant risks, both in terms of safety and the potential to alienate allies or create backlash, or your arrest and prosecution.

DIRECT ACTIONS INCLUDE:

- Physical occupations of key spaces
- Property destruction/targeting infrastructure: disrupt the normal functioning of the regime without causing harm to individuals, such as:
    - damaging surveillance cameras or blocking key government buildings with non-permanent barriers, or
    - parking and abandoning vehicles in the middle of important thoroughfares to create mass traffic jams.
- Symbolic property damage: create visual

disruptions and signal opposition to the regime without causing long-term harm:
- graffiti,
- breaking windows of state-owned businesses or institutions, or businesses known to support the state, or
- defacing monuments associated with the regime's power.

- Intentional mischief: small acts, teamed with many other small acts, add up. This can include:
  - mass mailings,
  - attending town meetings and creating minor disturbances,
  - ending emails and letters to people in power at their home addresses, or
  - shipping dog excrement to the offices of people in power,
  - going on a tour of the White House wearing some form of resistance t-shirt under your sweater, and then removing the sweater during the tour.
- Disruption of supply chains

While these actions may be effective in creating disruption and attracting attention, they always run the risk of escalating to violence, especially when a regime responds with force.

CHAPTER 7
DEMONSTRATIONS

Going to your first demonstration? This chapter is a comprehensive guide.

Safety Considerations

- Know your rights:
  - Familiarize yourself with the local laws regarding protests, assembly, and free speech. Understanding what you're legally allowed to do can prevent unnecessary conflict.
- Stay calm and non-violent:
  - Avoid engaging in violent behavior or confrontations with law enforcement or other protesters. Violence can escalate the situation, putting you and others at risk and detracting from the message you're trying to convey.
- Plan your exit:
  - Be aware of where you are and have a plan for leaving in case the situation becomes dangerous. Know alternative routes out of the area, and if possible, identify safe zones like public buildings or areas with a lot of people.

- Dress appropriately:
  - Wear comfortable clothing, sturdy shoes, and bring essentials like water and snacks. Avoid wearing anything that can easily identify you or make you a target (such as distinctive clothing or accessories).
- Protect your identity:
  - Depending on the political climate, it may be wise to take precautions to protect your identity. Consider wearing a mask or face covering if you're concerned about surveillance or retaliation.
- Stay in groups:
  - There's safety in numbers. Stick with friends or trusted allies, and make sure everyone has a way to contact each other during the demonstration.
- Document everything:
  - If it's safe to do so, document your participation with your phone or camera. Record any violations of rights or questionable actions that could be useful later.
- Follow official instructions:
  - If law enforcement provides instructions or warnings, take them seriously. Ignoring them can lead to arrests or escalation.
- Have a clear message:
  - Ensure the purpose of the protest is clear and concise. Whether it's through signs, chants, or speeches, a focused message helps build momentum and clarity.
- Engage the media:
  - If possible, engage with journalists or have someone designated as a spokesperson. The media can amplify your message, especially if

it's presented in a peaceful, organized manner.
- Know your target audience:
  - Consider who you want to influence (e.g., government officials, public opinion, specific groups) and adjust your approach to appeal to them. Tailor your messaging to resonate with your intended audience.
- Collaborate with other groups:
  - Partner with other organizations, activists, or communities who share your goals. Unity can increase the visibility and impact of your cause.
- Keep social media active:
  - Use social media to promote the demonstration, share live updates, and rally supporters. Just be mindful of privacy and security risks.
- Prepare for post-demonstration actions:
  - Protests are often just the beginning. Consider follow-up actions, whether through petitions, contacting lawmakers, or organizing future events. Keeping momentum going is key to ensuring that the demonstration leads to lasting change.

―――

Dos and Don'ts of Demonstrations

If you join a demonstration or participate in an act of civil disobedience, please be prepared.

First, **do *not* bring**:

- Anything illegal or questionable – no weapons, drugs, or contraband.
- Valuable items – bring only what you can afford to lose.

- Jewelry or identifiable accessories – keep your appearance low-profile.
- Contact lenses – tear gas can cause issues with them.

DO bring these:

- Water: preferably in a plastic bottle (some places don't allow metal).
- Snacks: high-energy, non-perishable food like protein bars, nuts, or dried fruit.
- ID & cash: keep a copy of your ID and some cash for emergencies (avoid credit/debit cards if possible).
- Emergency contact info – write numbers on paper (or on your arm) in case your phone is lost or confiscated.
- Medications: any essential prescription meds in original bottles, as loose pills might cause legal issues.
- First aid kit: bandages, antiseptic wipes, pain relievers, and any necessary medical supplies.
- Mask & goggles: N95 or similar mask to protect from tear gas, smoke, and airborne irritants; swim goggles for eye protection.
- Gloves: nonlatex gloves for protection from irritants or in case of injury.
- Hand sanitizer & wipes
- Tissues or bandana: can be used for wiping sweat, covering face, or handling items
- Comfortable, weather-appropriate clothes: dress in layers if needed.
- Sturdy shoes: wear closed-toe shoes or boots for protection.

- Hat & sunglasses to shield against sun and surveillance.
- Rain poncho or lightweight jacket: weather can change, and it can also serve as protection.
- Extra socks: in case of wet feet or long hours on the move.
- Legal information
    - Know your rights card – a printed guide on legal rights if detained (**see below**)
    - Lawyer's phone number – written on paper and possibly on your arm in case of arrest.
    - Emergency plan – arrange check-ins with a trusted person.
- Sharpie or permanent marker: to write important numbers on your body.
- Small notebook & pen to write down important details
- Duct tape: small roll for unexpected needs.
- Electronics & communication
    - Fully charged phone & battery pack: a backup power source is crucial.
        - A second phone is also useful for additional recording or to use for calls.
        - A burner phone is also useful to prevent confiscation of personal information.
    - Turn off fingerprint/face recognition: use a passcode for phone security.
    - If possible, remove any apps or information that could be used against you if your phone is confiscated.

KNOW YOUR RIGHTS – PROTESTER RIGHTS CARD

Bring this information with you to any demonstration and use if detained or arrested.

- **I am exercising my First Amendment right to peacefully protest.**
- **I have the right to remain silent.**
- **I choose to remain silent.**
- **I do not consent to a search of myself, my belongings, or my phone.**
- **I wish to speak to a lawyer before answering any questions.**
- **If I am not under arrest, I would like to leave. Am I free to go?**

REMEMBER:

- Stay calm and do not resist, even if your rights are violated.
- You have the right to record public officials, including the police.
- Do not lie to law enforcement or provide false documents.
- If detained, ask, "Am I being detained?" If not, walk away.
- If arrested, say "I want to remain silent and speak to a lawyer." Do not discuss your case with anyone other than your lawyer.
- You do NOT have to unlock your phone or provide passwords, but law enforcement may search your phone *if* they have a warrant.
- Use strong passwords and enable encryption on your devices.
- LEGAL HELP:_____(insert legal aid hotline, name, or phone number)

. . .

FINAL TIPS:

- Go with a group: there's safety in numbers.
- Memorize an emergency contact number in case your phone is lost.
- Stay sober & aware.
- Check for exit routes regularly, as conditions may change quickly.

CHAPTER 8
SEVEN WAYS TO COMMUNICATE WITH AUTHORITARIAN SUPPORTERS

During a demonstration, it is likely that you will encounter others who disagree with your message.

And, what if your neighbor, friend or family member supports the authoritarian regime?

Here are seven rules on how to communicate, de-escalate conflict, and live to fight another day.

ONE: RESPECT EVERYONE

- Don't look down on them, and don't patronize them, even if you know what they're saying has no factual basis or you find it offensive.
- Don't preach. Instead, ask questions.
- Try to understand where they are coming from, what their problems are, and why they see solutions to them in the regime.
- Treat them as people, as equals. They believe what they're saying is true and they might have valid reasons for their support.

Two: handle your emotions wisely

- Don't get emotional, and don't get provoked into heated arguments.
- Fight the other side's emotions with your calm, logical approach.
- The angrier they get, the calmer you should be. They'll calm down eventually.

Three: Think About What You Have In Common

- Focus on what you have in common.
- Do you live in the same neighborhood?
- Do you work in the same company or sector? The smaller the community, the easier it is. Give examples, like "We all need to get this done for all of us, if we don't cooperate neither of us will have it."

Four: be aware of what you say

- Use their language, don't treat it as inferior or below you – don't seem patronizing.
- If they curse, curse with them.
- If they approach you with humor, reply with humor.
- Show them you're actually not that different.
- As long as you communicate on two different planes, you will never meet.

Five: all information is useful

- Don't block their news sources, and don't turn away from their leaders and authority figures.

- Treat them as an insight to their worldview and tactics.
- Use them to your advantage, to better prepare for their arguments.
- Whenever you don't agree with something or detect a lie, voice it calmly, expose it with factual arguments.

Six: talk about policies, not people

- Pinpoint the practical, negative effects of their side's actions, ones that affect them directly.
- Find examples of how they, their families, children or friends will be personally impacted by their policies, or how it will affect your shared community.

Seven: be friendly

- If all else fails, don't turn away.
- Don't abandon your friends and family,
- Don't shun your neighbors,
- Remember, an authoritarian wants to divide you to control you.
- So, invite them over to your BBQ, crack open a beer, and who knows, maybe they'll realize you're not so different after all.

(from the Eastern European Twitter account of 2017)

CHAPTER 9
COMPREHENSIVE PLANS FOR DEMONSTRATION SAFETY

De-escalation: *prevent violence, protect yourself and others, and maintain the purpose of the demonstration.*
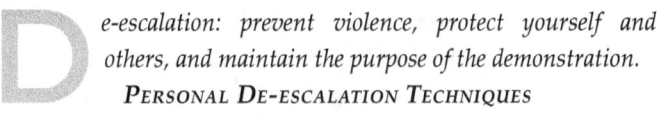

- Remain calm & non-threatening:
  - keep your voice even,
  - use non-aggressive body language, and
  - maintain a relaxed but alert posture.
  - Remember, if you engage in a violent act, it is likely that you will be met with violence in return.
- Avoid direct confrontation:
  - If tensions rise, step back, breathe, and defuse the situation with non-reactive behavior.
- Use neutral phrases. If confronted by an aggressive person, say:
  - "I hear you."
  - "We're all here for the same reason."
  - "I want to keep everyone safe, including you."
- Redirect attention:

- If violence seems likely, draw attention to a different action, chant, or group movement.
- Engage allies:
  - Call on nearby peaceful protesters to help mediate before things escalate.

Group De-escalation Strategies

- Appoint peacekeepers
  - Demonstrations often have designated peacekeepers to intervene in conflicts.
- Maintain space between groups
  - Avoid getting boxed in by hostile counter-protesters or aggressive authorities.
- Chant instead of shouting at individuals
  - Avoid direct verbal fights.
  - Organized chanting keeps focus on the message.
- Document conflicts
  - If tensions rise, video recording from a safe distance can protect against misinformation.

Interactions with Riot Police or Aggressive Authorities

- Do not run
  - Running can escalate a situation and may be seen as an admission of guilt.
- Stay together
  - Move as a unit and do not get separated from your group.
- Keep hands visible
  - Do not make sudden movements that could be interpreted as threatening.
- Comply without argument, then challenge legally

- Arguing with police in the moment rarely helps; legal challenges should be done later.

IN THE EVENT OF GUNFIRE:

- Seek cover
  - Move to an area where you are protected from direct line of sight or gunfire, such as behind vehicles, buildings, or any other structures that can shield you.
- Keep low to the ground
  - When you are in an open area, crouch or lie flat on the ground to minimize your exposure. Lowering your profile makes it harder for shooters to target you.
- Keep your hands visible
  - If the authorities are nearby, keep your hands visible at all times. This shows that you are not holding anything that could be perceived as a weapon.

IDENTIFY ESCAPE ROUTES IN ADVANCE

- Scout beforehand –
  - Before the demonstration, note:
    - Multiple exit routes (side streets, alleys, metro stations).
    - Nearby safe locations (hospitals, friendly businesses, legal aid offices).
    - Areas to avoid (police barricades, choke points).
- Have a meetup plan –
  - Set a rally point with friends in case you get separated.
- Use landmarks, not GPS

How to Exit Different Crisis Scenarios

1. Tear Gas or Other Chemical Weapons

- Tear gas in your eyes:
    - Leave the area immediately. As soon as you are exposed to tear gas, move away from the area of exposure, if possible, to avoid further inhalation of the gas or contact with other chemical agents.
    - Flush your eyes with water (or saline solution, if available). Tear gas is an irritant, and washing it out with cold water is the best way to provide immediate relief.
    - Do not rub your eyes. Rubbing your eyes can worsen the irritation and spread the chemicals.
- Tear gas on your skin:
    - Wash with soap and water as soon as possible. Avoid using alcohol or baby oil, as these can spread the chemical and make it worse.
- Inhaled tear gas:
    - Get fresh air
    - Cover your nose and mouth with a cloth (wet or dry) to help filter the gas. A wet bandana or towel over your mouth and nose can reduce inhalation.
    - Aftercare and monitoring:
        - If symptoms persist (for example, if you continue to have difficulty breathing, experience extreme pain in the eyes, or feel disoriented), it's important to seek medical

---

o In chaotic situations, your phone's signal may be blocked or jammed.

help immediately. Tear gas exposure can sometimes cause long-term irritation or respiratory issues, particularly if you have pre-existing conditions like asthma.

2. *Stampede or Crowd Surge*

- Move diagonally, not against the flow of the crowd.
- Protect your chest with your arms.
- If you fall, curl into a ball and protect your head until you can get up.

3. *Police Kettle (Encirclement)*

- If kettling is likely, leave early.
- If caught, remain calm and prepare for possible detention.

4. *Violent Clashes Nearby*

- Do not stay to observe.
- Walk, don't run, toward the nearest way out of the area.

CHAPTER 10
BYSTANDER INTERVENTION

BYSTANDER INTERVENTION TECHNIQUES AND REFERENCE GUIDES

Bystander intervention techniques refer to strategies you can use to intervene safely when you witness problematic behavior, such as bullying, harassment, or violence.

The goal is to prevent harm, de-escalate the situation, and ensure the well-being of those involved. Here are some suggestions:

- **Intervene directly** when you feel safe and confident that the situation can be resolved without escalating the conflict:
    - Approach the person who is being harmful or aggressive and calmly address the behavior.
    - For example, you could say, "That's not acceptable," or "Please stop."
    - In situations of police intervention during protests, direct intervention might not always be safe.
        - However, if you are in a position where you can calmly approach officers and ask

questions like, "What's going on here?" or "Is this necessary?" without being confrontational, it can sometimes de-escalate the situation.

- **Distract from the situation** when it doesn't feel safe to directly intervene:
  - Create a diversion by starting a conversation with someone else, asking a question, or doing something unexpected. This can interrupt the tension and provide an opportunity for the victim to escape.
  - If you see a situation escalating involving police, you might distract the officers by drawing attention to a different issue, such as helping a person who seems injured or drawing attention to a specific action of the police (such as an officer acting aggressively) that could stop the escalation.

- **Delegate intervention to someone else** if the situation is serious, you don't feel safe intervening, or you aren't sure how to handle it:
  - If you don't feel safe intervening directly, you can call someone who is in a position to step in or take responsibility, like a supervisor or the police, depending on the seriousness of the situation.
  - If you see an instance of police brutality or unnecessary force, you can contact legal observers, protest organizers, or human rights organizations that can document the event or get the attention of legal teams who can take further action. It's important to have contacts who can provide aid in case of police overreach.

- **Delay your intervention** if you're unable to intervene in the moment but want to ensure the person's well-being and offer help afterward:
  - Reach out to the individual who was targeted after the situation has passed to provide emotional support, validate their experience, and discuss options for further action, if necessary.

- **Seek support of others** when you're unsure about how to intervene, but there's safety in numbers or when collective action could be more effective:
  - Rally others to help either by intervening together or by supporting the person who is being harmed.
  - If you're observing police brutality, gathering witnesses or legal observers (who may be trained in how to handle these situations) can help ensure that there's documentation and support for those affected.
  - Some organizations may provide specific tools, such as a hotline to report police misconduct or legal support

- **Safety first!**
  - Always ensure your own safety before intervening in a situation.
  - Assess the environment and decide on the best course of action, which could involve authorities or finding ways to de-escalate without physical confrontation.
  - Ensure that you have a clear exit strategy if things go wrong.

DOCUMENTATION

If you cannot directly intervene, one of the most valuable ways to help is to document the situation. Record video footage or take photos (if it's safe to do so), ensuring that you capture important details like badge numbers or the identities of officers involved in potential misconduct. Videos can be crucial in holding authorities accountable.

KNOW YOUR RIGHTS

Understand what legal rights you have as a bystander. In some countries, recording police activity in public spaces is protected by law, but this varies. In the USA, taking photos or videos in public spaces is legal and protected as a First Amendment right; in some states, however, audio recording is not permitted. Knowing your rights can help you avoid unnecessary legal trouble while documenting or intervening.

CHAPTER 11
YOU AND THE LAW

If stopped, detained, or arrested, it's critical to know how to respond. Note: many of these items may be specific to the USA and not other countries.

IF STOPPED BY POLICE

- Stay calm & silent
- You have the right to record public officials, including the police.
- Do not lie to law enforcement or provide false documents.
- Say: "I am exercising my right to remain silent."
- Ask: "Am I free to go?"
- If they say no, ask: "Am I being detained?" If yes, ask why.
- Do not consent to a search
  - You can say: "I do not consent to a search."
- If they search you anyway, do not resist but repeat your lack of consent.
- Do not answer questions – anything you say can be used against you.
- Have your "Know Your Rights Card" ready.

- **IMPORTANT FOR DIGITAL PRIVACY**:
- You do NOT have to unlock your phone or provide passwords.
- Law enforcement may search your phone only if they have a warrant.
- Use strong passwords and enable encryption on your devices.

IF YOU ARE ARRESTED

- Do not resist: even if the arrest is unlawful, resisting makes it worse.
- Ask for a lawyer immediately: do not answer questions without one.
- Remember details: note badge numbers, officer descriptions, and what was said.

IF YOU WITNESS SOMEONE ELSE BEING ARRESTED

- Record video If possible: be discreet and upload immediately to social media if possible.
- Chant supportively.
  - Phrases like "Let them go!" or "We are watching!" can help.
- Share arrest details with legal observers: write down what you see and report to legal aid groups.

WHAT HAPPENS IF YOU ARE ARRESTED?

Common charges and consequences for protest arrests can include the following:

- Disorderly Conduct (a.k.a. Disturbing the Peace)
  - This is a broad charge that covers blocking traffic, making excessive noise, or failing to disperse when ordered.

- Consequences: usually a misdemeanor, with possible fines or short jail time (often a few days or community service).
- Unlawful Assembly
  - Applied when authorities declare a protest illegal (e.g., for not having a permit or turning violent).
  - Consequences: typically, a misdemeanor, with possible fines and probation. In rare cases, jail time up to a year.
- Failure to Disperse
  - If law enforcement orders a crowd to leave and someone remains, they may be arrested.
  - Consequences: misdemeanor, leading to fines or brief jail time.
- Trespassing
  - Entering or remaining on private or restricted public property without permission.
  - Consequences: misdemeanor, punishable by fines, community service, or jail (usually up to a few months).
- Resisting Arrest (or Obstructing an Officer)
  - Even passive resistance, such as sitting down or refusing to put hands behind the back, can lead to this charge.
  - Consequences: can be a misdemeanor or felony, depending on the level of resistance. Jail time and fines vary.
- Vandalism (Destruction of Property)
  - Includes graffiti, damaging buildings, breaking windows, or spray-painting signs.
  - Consequences: if damage is minor, it's a misdemeanor with fines; if significant, it can be a felony with jail time.
- Curfew Violation

- Some cities impose curfews during protests, and violating them can lead to arrest.
- Consequences: usually a minor offense, but can result in fines or community service.
- Riot or Inciting a Riot
  - If authorities believe someone is encouraging violence or destruction, they may charge them with incitement.
  - Consequences: this can be a felony in some jurisdictions, leading to serious penalties, including years in prison.

Booking & Detention

After arrest, individuals are fingerprinted, photographed, and held.

Some may be released quickly, while others may wait for a court appearance.

Bail or release: many misdemeanor offenses qualify for release without bail, while felony charges may require bail or a court hearing.

Potential Penalties

- Fines range from $50 to several thousand dollars, depending on the charge.
- Jail Time:
  - Misdemeanors: up to one year (often less).
- Felonies:
  - Years in prison, though usually only for violent offenses.
- Probation or community service often given instead of jail.
- Permanent criminal record:
  - Some misdemeanor charges can stay on record for life, affecting jobs, housing, and travel.
- Expungement may be possible for minor offenses.

Defense Strategies

- If arrested, possible defenses include:
- First Amendment Protection
  - Peaceful protest is a constitutional right (though not absolute—it can be limited for safety concerns).
- Unlawful Arrest
  - If law enforcement failed to issue clear dispersal orders or acted outside legal boundaries.
- Lack of Evidence
  - If there is no proof that the arrested person committed the act (e.g., resisting arrest).
- Selective Enforcement
  - If arrests target certain people unfairly, this can be challenged in court.

Should You Get a Lawyer?

For misdemeanors, a public defender may be enough. For felonies, or if concerned about a permanent record, hiring a defense lawyer is recommended.

Some legal aid organizations provide pro bono defense for protesters. For more information, check (in the USA) with organizations like American Civil Liberties Union (ACLU) and Rocket Lawyer.

CHAPTER 12
RESILIENCE AND REPAIR

Activists must be able to cope with fear, doubt, disappointment, and possible physical and moral injury, while staying committed to the cause.

Know when you are tired, or demoralized, and take a break.

Quick reminders:

- Control your anger: count to ten before responding to or doing something that could harm yourself or others.
- In general, if you do something violent, you will be met with violence in return.
- Calculate what you can endure, and whether your actions will ultimately benefit the common good.
- Before getting involved in any act of resistance, no matter how small, remember these simple practices to increase your resilience:
    - Ground yourself and calm yourself
    - Remember your intentions for being involved
    - Attune yourself to your surroundings, others, and yourself

- Consider what will be the best course of action in the moment
- End the action gracefully and as completely as possible, leaving it behind at the end of the day, or later, talking about it with others.

KEY ELEMENTS OF PSYCHOLOGICAL RESILIENCE

- Build a sense of purpose
  - When people understand the higher purpose behind their actions—whether it's justice, freedom, or equality—they are more likely to stay engaged and committed.
  - Fighting *against* a repressive regime must be coupled with fighting *for* the things you value, and effecting positive change.
- Solidarity and social support
  - People who feel part of a larger cause are less likely to give up or be swayed by fear.
- Normalize risk
  - Activists must be prepared for the risks they face, both physical and psychological.
- Self-care and emotional health
  - It is important for activists to engage in self-care and support each other through difficult times.
  - Providing spaces for people to process their emotions, share their struggles, and take care of their mental health helps to sustain the movement.
  - Use recognized tools to help maintain well-being in the aftermath of potentially traumatic circumstances, such as
    - Critical Incident Stress Debriefing,
    - EFT ("tapping" or Emotional Freedom Technique)

- EMDR (for more involved therapeutic work) and other methods of identifying and defusing the effects of traumatic events in the body and mind.

Immediate Methods for Care of Self and Others After a Demonstration

Engaging in all forms of civil disobedience can be either immediately traumatic or cause you to feel triggered from past traumatic events.

It is important and possible to identify when one enters a triggered or shocked state, and then to begin releasing it and healing from it as quickly as possible.

Typical trauma reactions fall into categories you may be able to recognize in yourself: the fight, flight, and freeze responses.

Example: you witness a violent event during a demonstration, in which someone is beaten and is bleeding badly. You stand in place, staring, and feel unable to move. For an hour afterwards, you feel tight and compressed inside, barely able to speak. This is a kind of "freeze" response.

The body naturally holds onto energy after a traumatic event, and by engaging in movement or specific practices immediately, you can help your nervous system reset and restore balance.

Here are some methods that can help you in the short term to recover from critical incidents, whether you observed them happen or experienced them yourself.

- Jumping or Shaking
  - Jumping, shaking, or even dancing are all ways to help the body release the energy of trauma and move from a state of frozen, immobilized energy into one of fluidity and safety.
- Breath of Fire

- This is a yoga-based breathing exercise. Sit or stand up straight, then inhale and exhale rapidly through the nose while keeping the mouth closed. The inhale should be short, and the exhale should be forceful. Aim for about 1-2 breaths per second. Start slowly and increase intensity. It can help release tension.
- Body Movement / Large Muscle Activation
    - Moving the big muscles of the body can be incredibly helpful. In "Somatic Experiencing" therapy, large muscle movement can help release tension and fear. Walking, running, jumping jacks, or even using a foam roller to gently massage large muscle groups are helpful.
- Sighing or Vocalizing
    - Sighing or making vocal sounds (such as humming or even yelling in a safe environment) can also help release the tension held in the body. Trauma can create a kind of "stuck" energy in the throat and chest area, and vocalizing or sighing can help discharge this energy.
- Use of Weighted Blankets or Firm Touch
    - Sometimes, providing deep touch pressure or feeling "held" can activate the parasympathetic nervous system, helping to counteract the stress response and promote relaxation.
    - Weighted blankets can be helpful
    - You might also practice "self-holding," by placing your hands gently on your arms, chest, or legs, offering yourself a sense of nurturing care.
    - Alternatively, you and your team can take turns hugging and/or applying gentle pressure on

each other: one person lies on the ground, while the others simply press firmly (but not forcefully) on the person's legs, torso, arms, and head.
- Yoga and Stretching
    - Many yoga poses are specifically designed to release tension from the body and increase flexibility, which can be helpful after trauma.
    - Poses such as Child's Pose, Forward Fold, or even standing poses like Warrior or Mountain Pose can support emotional grounding.
- Tapping (EFT – Emotional Freedom Technique)
    - Tapping involves gently tapping on specific acupressure points on the body, often while speaking about or focusing on the traumatic experience. How to practice tapping:
    - Using the pads of your fingers, tap on acupressure points on your body, such as on your head, face, chest, and under the arms, while focusing on your feelings of distress. You might say phrases like "Even though I feel shaken and overwhelmed, I am safe now," as you tap.
- 5, 4, 3, 2, 1 Grounding
    - Name 5 things you can see
        - Take a moment to spot five things in your immediate environment. Whether it's a basic office chair or a cherished family photo, the goal is to really see the details—like color, form, and texture. By diverting your focus to your sense of sight, you disrupt the cycle of anxious or stressful thoughts.
    - Name 4 things you can hear
        - Close your eyes and listen to the ambient noises around you. They could be anything

from a fan humming to birds singing, or people talking in the distance. Identifying these sounds helps steer your mind away from inward worries and more toward the world around you, anchoring you in the present moment.
- Name 3 things you can feel
  - Concentrate on the sense of touch to further ground yourself. Become aware of three things you can feel. They could be the fabric of your clothes against your skin, the texture of an item you're holding, or the solidity of the floor under your feet.
- Name 2 things you can smell
  - Take a deep breath and identify two distinct smells around you. They could be the welcoming aroma of fresh coffee or the clean scent of hand soap. Tuning into these smells helps shift your focus from looping thoughts to your immediate surroundings, reinforcing your connection to the present moment.
- Name 1 thing you can taste
  - Finally, focus on your sense of taste. You might want to take a sip of water, or simply focus on the lingering flavor of toothpaste in your mouth. Centering on this final sense completes the cycle and firmly brings you back to the present moment.

- Cold Water Treatment for Panic Attacks
  - If you feel one coming on, try this practical way to use cold water for anxiety. Dunk your face in cold water while holding your breath for 15-30 seconds. This reduces blood flow to non-essential organs and instead focuses blood to

the brain and heart — reducing panic symptoms. Or:
- Hold an ice cube in your hand and focus on the sensation
- Place a cold, wet washcloth on the back of your neck
- Dunk your head into a bowl of ice water

All of the above can be practiced alone or in a group.

It is wise for a group leader to suggest a debriefing session after any act of civil disobedience, which could include any of the methods suggested above.

Debriefing, group yoga, grounding, EFT, and so on, as a group, can also help the group remember the power of their movement and their cause, and refuel morale, hope and purpose when times are challenging.

The goal is to help the body discharge trauma without overwhelming the nervous system further.

However, if you're struggling after a traumatic event, it's always best to seek support from a trained therapist who is well-schooled in working with trauma and critical incidents.

———

INSPIRING HOPE AND MAINTAINING MORALE

The regime may attempt to demoralize the people by making the struggle seem futile, but a key psychological tactic of rebellion is to keep hope alive and remind people that their efforts matter. Do this through:

- Celebrate the Visible Victories:
    - Even small victories—such as the resignation of a government official, a successful protest, or

the defection of a high-ranking officer—can have a significant impact on morale.
    - These victories should be highlighted and celebrated, showing the people that their efforts are not in vain and that change is possible.

- Reframe the Narrative:
    - It is essential to challenge the narrative put forth by the regime. Revolutionaries must frame their struggle as a fight for justice, rights, and human dignity, emphasizing the moral high ground they occupy.
        - By highlighting the regime's corruption, violence, and illegitimacy, resistance movements can rally people around the idea that they are on the right side of history.

- Use Symbols of Resistance:
    - Symbols, slogans, and metaphors can be powerful tools for maintaining morale. They serve as reminders of the movement's values and purpose, and they help activists stay focused on the larger goal.
    - For example, the raised fist is a symbol of resistance and solidarity that has been used in many struggles, from the Civil Rights Movement in the U.S. to the anti-apartheid movement in South Africa.

- Humanize the Struggle:
    - The movement should continuously humanize its cause by sharing personal stories of resistance, suffering, and resilience.

- Stories of individual acts of bravery, even in the face of extreme adversity, help to build a sense of collective strength and remind participants that they are part of a larger, meaningful fight.

MLK 1963 Washington March, Warren K. Leffler

CHAPTER 13
CREATIVE RESISTANCE: A SHORT HISTORY OF CREATIVE ACTS OF REBELLION

Here are some notable examples of unique actions that challenged oppressive regimes.

The Rosenstrasse Protest, (Germany, 1943)

In 1943, hundreds of non-Jewish German women defied the Nazi regime. They demanded the release of their Jewish husbands who had been incarcerated by the Gestapo. They showed how ordinary people can become heroes by defying authority and taking risks, day by day.

- Hundreds of women gathered together outside Rosenstrasse 2-4 and refused to leave until their husbands were released.
- The Minister of Propaganda, Josef Goebbels, placed a complete media blackout on the protest and planned to have them arrested or shot. However, he was aware that arresting or harming such a large group of German women might be problematic.
- So, he simply decided to let the Jews go. His rationale was that it would have been better to quell the protest ensure that it didn't spread to other places around the Reich.

The Velvet Revolution (Czechoslovakia, 1989)

The Velvet Revolution in Czechoslovakia was a peaceful resistance movement that culminated in the overthrow of the communist regime in 1989. The revolution was largely non-violent and relied heavily on large, peaceful demonstrations.

- One of the most colorful aspects of the revolution was the widespread use of art, theatre, and music in protests.
- Protesters used symbolic gestures such as wearing velvet scarves and other soft fabrics, which were an elegant and non-confrontational symbol of resistance.
- The velvet symbolized the peaceful and gentle nature of the revolution, contrasting sharply with the violence often associated with overthrowing regimes.

The Salt March (India, 1930)

Led by Mahatma Gandhi, the Salt March was a key act of civil disobedience during India's struggle for independence from British colonial rule.

- The British government had a monopoly on the production of salt in India, and Gandhi organized a 240-mile march to the coastal town of Dandi to produce salt illegally from the sea.
- What made the Salt March particularly colorful was the symbolism it carried. It was not just a protest against the salt tax but a powerful act of non-violent resistance.
- Thousands of followers, including women and children, marched alongside Gandhi, each of them becoming part of the symbolic defiance. Gandhi's act of making salt from the sea represented self-

reliance and defied the authority of the British Empire.
- The Salt March became one of the most iconic non-violent protests in history and played a key role in India gaining independence in 1947.

The White Rose Movement (Nazi Germany, 1942–1943)

The White Rose was a resistance group in Nazi Germany, primarily made up of students and a professor from the University of Munich. The group's most famous action was distributing leaflets that denounced the Nazi regime and called for peaceful resistance.

- They printed and spread leaflets with simple but powerful messages, sometimes featuring flowers, particularly the white rose, as their symbol of peace and resistance against the tyranny of the Nazi regime.
- Although the group was eventually discovered and members executed, their actions remain a powerful example of intellectual resistance and the use of symbolism in protest.
- The White Rose's use of the white rose as a symbol of purity, hope, and non-violence became iconic in the history of resistance movements.

Pussy Riot (Russia, 2012)

Pussy Riot is a feminist punk rock group based in Russia, known for their bold and often controversial performances aimed at protesting Russian political and social issues.

- Their most famous action took place in Moscow's Christ the Savior Cathedral in 2012 when they performed a punk prayer in protest against the

Russian Orthodox Church's support for President Vladimir Putin.
- The performance was highly colorful, with members wearing brightly-colored balaclavas and neon tights.
- The protest was an unexpected and stark visual contrast to the religious setting, making it both shocking and attention-grabbing.
- Their act was as much about art and performance as it was about political protest, incorporating a playful yet forceful approach to expressing dissent.
- While several members were arrested and sentenced to prison, their actions sparked a global conversation about free speech, the role of women in politics, and the limits of protest under authoritarian regimes.
- The group's use of bright colors and symbolic masks became a globally recognized form of resistance.

The Umbrella Movement (Hong Kong, 2014)

The Umbrella Movement in Hong Kong was a series of pro-democracy protests that took place in 2014, demanding universal suffrage and the right to freely elect leaders.

- The movement is named after the yellow umbrellas that protesters used to shield themselves from pepper spray and tear gas deployed by the police.
- The color yellow was used to represent hope and solidarity, and the umbrellas quickly became a visual emblem of the protest.
- Protesters also used creative methods like occupying streets and public spaces, forming human chains, and setting up tent cities in public squares.

- While the Umbrella Movement did not achieve its immediate political goals, it drew significant international attention to Hong Kong's political struggles and became a symbol of youth-led resistance in Asia. The umbrellas and yellow color scheme became synonymous with non-violent protest.

The Chilean "Pancake Protest" (2011)

In 2011, Chile experienced massive student protests demanding education reform. The "pancake protest" was a unique and playful form of resistance against the government's education policies.

- The protest involved students cooking pancakes in public spaces to symbolize how the education system was "flipping" their future upside down.
- The colorful pancakes were distributed to passersby, along with flyers about the protesters' demands. The playful nature of the protest helped to capture the attention of the media and public.
- The protest garnered international attention for its creativity and humor, making a serious political point through an unexpected and lighthearted approach. It demonstrated how humor and unusual symbolism could be powerful tools in raising awareness about social issues.

The "Women in Black" (Various Countries)

Women in Black is an international feminist peace movement that was founded in 1988 in Israel and has since spread to other countries. The group conducts silent vigils and protests against violence, war, and human rights violations.

- The women stand in silent vigil, often wearing black clothing as a symbol of mourning and resistance.
- Their silence and the uniformity of their appearance give their protests a strong visual impact, with the color black symbolizing opposition to violence and the struggle for peace.
- The group's simple but powerful use of black clothing and silence has made their protests instantly recognizable and a strong visual reminder of the need for peace and justice. Their actions have inspired similar movements in many parts of the world, demonstrating the power of non-verbal protest.

The "Candlelight Movement" (South Korea, 2002 and 2016)

South Korea's Candlelight Movement is a series of large-scale protests where people took to the streets holding candles to express opposition to government corruption, authoritarianism, and human rights abuses.

- The use of candles as a protest tool became a strong visual and symbolic act of peaceful dissent. The soft glow of candles represented a gentle resistance against oppressive regimes, while the act of holding candles together in the dark symbolized the power of collective action and the hope for a better future.
- The Candlelight Movement was crucial in bringing down President Park Geun-hye in 2017 due to her corruption scandal, demonstrating how peaceful yet powerful visual symbolism can mobilize large numbers of people and force political change.

The "Tiananmen Square Protest" (China, 1989)

One of the most iconic and colorful moments in modern

resistance movements came from the Tiananmen Square protests in China. In the face of a violent crackdown by the Chinese government, a lone protester stood in front of a line of tanks, blocking their path.

- The image of the "Tank Man"—a man standing in front of a column of tanks holding grocery bags—became an icon of peaceful resistance.
- The powerful symbolism of a lone individual facing down military might captured the world's attention, despite efforts by the Chinese government to suppress media coverage.
- While the protest was violently suppressed, the image of Tank Man remains one of the most poignant symbols of resistance against oppression in the modern era.

Smartphone App Appropriation (ongoing)

Appropriate a politically neutral phone application to your cause by overwhelming it with campaign messages.

Ingenious users of common apps increasingly are organizing to leverage these platforms to spotlight an injustice, embarrass a target, or change how the public understands an issue.

- In Russia, people under lockdown reappropriated a popular app typically used to monitor road traffic to protest their government's mishandling of the COVID-19 pandemic.
- *Lesbians and Gays Support the Migrants,* a UK group, created right-swiping Tinder bots to enlighten app users on British Airways' complicit role in deportations.

CHAPTER 14
USING PSYCHOLOGICAL TACTICS AGAINST THE REGIME

By exploiting the regime's vulnerabilities and creating confusion or doubt within its ranks, resistance movements can weaken the power of the oppressors without resorting to violence.

- Expose the regime's corruption
    - The psychological impact of corruption is significant, both for the regime itself and for its supporters.
    - By continuously exposing the regime's corrupt practices, human rights violations, and abuses of power, resistance movements can create a psychological burden on the regime's officials, making them question the legitimacy of their own actions.

- Disrupt the regime's unity
    - Authoritarian regimes often rely on unity within their ranks to maintain control.
    - Resistance movements can exploit divisions between elites, factions within the military or

police, and cracks within the regime's leadership.
- Encouraging defections, exposing internal disagreements, and creating a sense of instability within the regime's power structure can weaken its ability to function.

- Create cognitive dissonance
  - Cognitive dissonance occurs when people are confronted with information that contradicts their beliefs or actions, leading to psychological discomfort.
  - Resistance movements can exploit cognitive dissonance by presenting the regime's actions as unjust, illegal, or morally reprehensible.
  - This forces regime supporters to question their involvement and may lead to defections or internal conflicts.

- Use paradox and contradiction
  - For example, acts of radical compassion, such as offering food to the enemy or peacefully occupying a space that symbolizes oppressive power, have the potential to disarm the opposition and create unexpected opportunities for dialogue and transformation.

- Bring flowers to a march, not rocks, and pass them out to the police you encounter.

- Humor and satire
  - Humor and satire can be powerful tools in psychological warfare.
  - Laughter can provide a psychological release

from the stresses of resistance, helping activists cope with fear and pressure.
- Additionally, humor can be used to ridicule the regime and expose its absurdities, weakening its authority and making it appear less powerful and more vulnerable.

Vietnam Protests, 1968, photo by Bernie Boston

CHAPTER 15
DISRUPT THE REGIME'S SUPPLY CHAIN

One active way to challenge an authoritarian regime is to disrupt its ability to support itself (its "supply chain").

The supply chain can include everything from the delivery of physical, tangible items (such as the nuts and bolts necessary to build a warplane), to the people, organizations, or businesses that support the regime (its so-called "human capital").

Strategic economic, logistical, and digital disruption can cause long-term instability and push the government to change. Here are the steps a resistance group might take.

Supply Chain Sabotage – Key Points

Step 1: Identify weak points → Find the regime's biggest vulnerabilities.

Step 2: Use nonviolent disruptions first → Strikes, boycotts, logistical blockades.

Step 3: Leverage cyber & financial sabotage → Digital disruption, bank runs, misinformation.

Step 4: Consider targeted sabotage (as a last resort) → Fuel supply, railways, power grids.

Step 5: Maintain movement security → Encryption, decentralization, anonymity.

Step 6: Adapt & escalate as needed → Start small, then scale up if necessary.

IDENTIFY THE MOST VULNERABLE SUPPLY CHAIN LINKS

Not all industries or infrastructure are equally important to a regime. Focus on disrupting sectors that:

- Generate revenue (oil, gas, mining, state-controlled industries).
- Enable repression (military, police, surveillance systems).
- Ensure daily function (transport, electricity, banking, communications).

ORGANIZE NONVIOLENT DISRUPTIONS FIRST

Nonviolent tactics should be prioritized because they:

- Minimize risk of government retaliation.
- Gain public and international support.
- Can be executed by ordinary people without special training.

STRIKES

- Strikes slow down regime-critical industries without direct confrontation.
- Identify vulnerable industries (oil, transport, manufacturing, government offices).
- Secure worker commitment in secret (via underground networks, encrypted chat apps).
- Organize rolling strikes (different sectors stop working in phases to prolong impact).
- Provide support networks (food, money) so workers can sustain the strike.

Mass Boycotts

- Boycotts drain financial resources by reducing public cooperation with regime-linked businesses
- Identify state-owned businesses (banks, supermarkets, gas stations, Trump businesses, businesses of Republican or Project 2025 individuals).
- Spread the boycott message through stickers, graffiti, anonymous social media posts.
- Boycott banks and explore alternative funds.
  - Encourage people to withdraw cash, causing liquidity crises.
  - Overwhelm tax offices to delay regime revenue collection.
  - Use cryptocurrency or underground economies to weaken reliance on state banks.

Block Transportation & Logistics

- Organize sit-ins & human blockades at key intersections, ports, and train tracks.
- Encourage truckers & transport workers to refuse service to state-run institutions.
- Use misinformation to force evacuations and delays.
- Launch a "sick-out" protest (where workers call in sick en masse to halt operations).
- Encourage civil servants to "lose" important paperwork.
- Delete property or tax records.

Digital & Cyber Sabotage

Cyber sabotage is low-risk but highly effective in

disrupting authoritarian control. This is specialized work, but it can be learned via many online sources.

Hacking & Digital Disruption

- Overload government websites with mass traffic (DDoS attacks).
- Tamper with logistics databases (e.g., alter train schedules, fuel shipments).
- Leak sensitive information about corruption, military plans, or secret accounts.
- Disable surveillance networks (e.g., disrupt CCTV systems in protest areas)

"Human Capital" Supply Chain Disruption: Breaking the Workforce

Disrupting the human capital supply chain of an authoritarian regime means cutting off its ability to recruit, retain, and utilize the people who sustain it.

This includes government officials, military personnel, security forces, skilled professionals, and even laborers who support regime-controlled industries.

"Disruptions" can be demonstrations, blockades, and any sort of creative activity that has the effect of confusing or diminishing the functioning of the activities of people who support the regime.

- A small movement does not need weapons or massive resources to weaken an authoritarian regime's human capital. Instead, it can:
- Undermine morale through psychological pressure.
- Make regime jobs unappealing through economic and social costs.
- Stop recruitment by educating young people.
- Turn insiders into quiet saboteurs who slow down the system.

- Encourage defections and help workers escape.
- Target the weakest links, rather than fight the whole system.

Disrupt Recruitment & Training Pipelines

- Authoritarian regimes rely on a constant supply of new personnel to maintain control. Cutting off this flow weakens their long-term ability to govern.

Sabotage Military & Police Recruitment

- Discourage students from entering regime-critical fields (military academies, state media, government bureaucracy).

Promote Mass Avoidance Tactics if Conscription Is At Stake

- Encourage draft evasion through legal loopholes.
- Spread information on how to avoid conscription.
- Support family-based resistance to recruitment.

Destabilize Internal Loyalty Networks

- Many regimes maintain power through networks of loyalty, where bureaucrats, military officers, and business elites receive privileges in exchange for their support.
- Create internal fractures
- Expose cases of favoritism and corruption to make mid-level officials feel undervalued.
- Spread rumors and intelligence leaks that create paranoia among leadership.

- Encourage internal rivalries within different factions of the regime.

UNDERMINE ELITE MORALE

- Highlight the failures of the regime and its leadership.
- Spread information about luxurious lifestyles of top officials while lower ranks suffer.
- Encourage disillusionment among younger officials.

CREATE ECONOMIC HARDSHIPS FOR THE WORKFORCE

By disrupting the economic incentives that keep people working for the regime, you can push them to seek alternative employment or rebel.

- Encouraging strikes & work slowdowns
- Secretly organize labor movements within key industries.
- Provide financial support for workers who refuse to participate in regime activities.
- Destroying public trust in state institutions
- Expose lies about economic stability and job security.
- Spread awareness of alternative ways to earn income outside of regime control.

EXPOSE CORRUPTION & PRIVILEGE

Expose corruption & privilege in individuals or entities that benefit from the authoritarian regime:

- If the individual or business entity (the Trump Organization or SpaceX for example) benefits from

illicit gains (e.g., luxury properties, nepotistic business deals), highlighting these excesses could be effective.
- Activists could focus on exposing these privileges, through nonviolent demonstrations outside their places of business or residence.

Psychological Disengagement: Undermining Loyalty & Morale

Most people working for a regime do so out of habit, fear, or financial necessity, although some may also be motivated by ideological commitment.

A movement can erode their sense of duty by:

- Creating doubt about the regime's future,
- Spreading credible rumors about internal instability, purges, or financial decline,
- Publicizing high-profile defections to make staying seem riskier than leaving,
- Circulating leaked documents or testimonies that expose internal corruption,
- Sharing stories of defectors who explain why they left and how life improved,
- Highlighting the regime's abuses against its own lower-tier employees (e.g., military conscripts, bureaucrats, police officers).
- Using social media to appeal to insiders' doubts rather than attack them personally,
- Highlighting how low-level officials are often overworked and underpaid,
- Publishing salary comparisons showing how elites benefit while regular workers struggle,
- Revealing how top officials exploit their own subordinates (e.g., using them as personal servants).

Examples:

1. *A movement in Eastern Europe created anonymous Telegram channels where disgruntled police officers could discuss their frustrations safely, leading to mass resignations.*
2. *In Venezuela, activists used online leaks to expose that mid-level military officers were being paid in near-worthless currency while top generals lived in luxury. This increased dissatisfaction within the ranks.*

Turn Employees into Saboteurs

Not everyone inside a regime is loyal. One can infiltrate or convert regime employees into passive saboteurs by:

- Encouraging work slowdowns & bureaucratic sabotage,
- Convincing civil servants to "strictly follow procedures" to slow down government efficiency,
- Persuading workers to "lose" paperwork or misfile important documents,
- Encouraging sympathetic officials to leak information about corruption or abuses.

Make Regime Jobs Unattractive

Make working for the regime more costly and less rewarding by:

- Discouraging public cooperation with regime employees
- Refusing services (e.g., restaurants, shops) to known regime enforcers.
    - *Example: restaurants in Washington, DC, could refuse to serve known DOGE employees*

- Encouraging landlords to refuse to rent to regime workers (without targeting families).
- Denying participation in social or professional circles (clubs, events, etc.).

CHAPTER 16
NARRATIVE WARFARE

Work against the regime's "storyline" through these steps:

DEFINE THE COUNTER-NARRATIVE

1. Clearly identify the regime's dominant narrative (it's way of portraying itself) and find weaknesses.
    - Establish a simple, emotionally powerful alternative narrative, such as
        - "Freedom over Fear,"
        - "Truth vs. Lies"

2. Build a Decentralized Information Network
    - Use secure, censorship-resistant communication
        - Encrypted messaging apps (Signal, Telegram, Session)
        - Dark web & blockchain-based news platforms to avoid take-downs
        - Establish distributed leadership (no single point of failure)

- Use mirror sites & backup servers to resist censorship

3. Weaponize Social Media & Memes
    - Dominate hashtags:
        - Flood social media with trending protest slogans & viral images.
    - Meme Warfare:
        - Create humorous & emotional memes to spread resistance ideas.
        - Use satire to mock the regime (authoritarians hate being ridiculed).
        - Swarm regime propaganda accounts with counter-messaging.

4. Leak Information & Expose Corruption
    - Gather whistleblower leaks (insider corruption, classified documents).
    - Publish on WikiLeaks-style platforms or through trusted journalists.
    - Use "Dead Man's Switch" releases (pre-scheduled leaks in case of arrests).

6. Bypass Censorship & Reach International Media
    - Use VPNs & proxies to spread content.
    - Distribute physical media (USB drives, QR codes, printouts) in areas with internet blackouts.
    - Leak stories to independent journalists & foreign press to attract global attention.

6. Disrupt Regime Propaganda
    - Counter fake news: fact-check and debunk official government lies.

- Hijack propaganda events (turn staged celebrations into resistance moments).
- Dox corrupt officials: leak personal details of regime enforcers to make them accountable. (*See detailed instructions below*)

7. Prepare for Repression & Adapt
    - Have fallback channels: if Telegram is blocked, for example, switch to Matrix, Briar, or Signal.
    - Train members to avoid tracking.
    - Rotate protest strategies to stay unpredictable.
    - Encrypt all sensitive communications to prevent infiltration.

"Doxxing" and How to Do It

Doxxing (short for "document dropping") refers to the act of publicly revealing private or personally identifiable information (PII) about individuals, often without their consent.

This can include names, addresses, phone numbers, social media accounts, financial records, or employment details.

Doxxing police and government officials is a tactic used to:

- Expose corruption, misconduct, or brutality:
    - Releasing information on police officers involved in excessive force, political oppression, or human rights violations.
- Intimidate or apply public pressure:
    - Holding officials accountable by making them personally identifiable.

- Encourage direct action:
  - In some cases, activists dox individuals to target them with protests, legal complaints, or online harassment.

Doxxing is illegal in many countries, especially when used to incite harm or harassment. While some see it as a tool for accountability, others view it as a violation of privacy.

Those who engage in doxxing may themselves become targets of counter-doxxing by opposition groups.

CHAPTER 17
SPREADING INFORMATION WITHOUT GETTING CAUGHT

Spreading information safely is the lifeblood of resistance movements. The key is to:

- Be creative → Mix traditional and digital tactics.
- Stay anonymous → Use encryption, offline methods, and misdirection.
- Rotate strategies → Avoid patterns that authorities can track.
- Empower insiders → Whistleblowers and defectors can provide crucial intelligence.

Below are detailed strategies for achieving this, from graffiti to QR codes.

Using Graffiti and Anonymous Street Art to Share Messages

Graffiti and public messaging are effective, low-tech ways to reach the public without relying on digital networks that can be monitored.

What to Write?

- Short, powerful slogans (e.g., "Freedom is coming," "No to dictatorship").
- QR codes leading to underground media (e.g., Telegram channels, websites).
- Humorous or satirical messages that mock the regime (e.g., caricatures of leaders).
- Mysterious or coded symbols to create curiosity and unity among dissidents.

Where to Paint?

- Near government offices → Forces officials to see public dissent daily.
- On abandoned buildings → Less likely to be immediately removed.
- Inside public restrooms → Hidden, but seen by many people.
- At transport hubs → Metro stations, bus stops, and railways maximize exposure.

How to Avoid Getting Caught

- Use quick-dry spray paint or stickers (5-second application time).
- Work in teams (one lookout, one painter, one person recording for proof).
- Wear gloves and cover faces (to avoid fingerprinting and surveillance).
- Change locations frequently (never hit the same place twice in a row).
- Use pre-made stencils to paint quickly and reduce time at the scene.

Spreading Documents with Flash Drives or QR Codes

Flash drives and QR codes are offline methods to share information securely and anonymously.

Using Flash Drives (USB Drop Tactic)

Since many people still use USB drives, they can be used to distribute:

- Anti-regime books, articles, and pamphlets,
- Videos exposing government corruption,
- Apps and VPN software for secure internet access.

How to Drop USBs Safely

- Leave them in public places (libraries, internet cafés, university desks).
- Label them as something else (e.g., "Free Music" or "Business Reports" to encourage use).
- Use cheap, disposable drives (avoid connecting them to your personal devices).
- Encrypt contents with a simple unlock code (e.g., "Freedom2025").

Example: In North Korea, defectors smuggle USBs with South Korean movies, news reports, and educational materials to undermine government propaganda.

QR Codes for Anonymous Information Sharing

QR codes are an effective way to direct people to websites, Telegram channels, or digital manifestos without writing full URLs (which can be censored).

How to Use QR Codes Safely:

- Print stickers or flyers with QR codes leading to underground websites.
- Embed QR codes into public murals, posters, or everyday objects.
- Make QR codes small enough to be overlooked by authorities but recognizable to activists.
- Rotate links frequently so that authorities cannot block them all at once.

Example: Activists in Russia's anti-Putin movement placed QR code stickers in public places that led to information about protests, bypassing censorship.

Even if the regime controls the internet, information can still be spread by:

- Handwritten notes and letters → old-school, but hard to track.
- Handing out flyers in crowded areas → distribute quickly and walk away.
- Word of mouth via trusted networks → best for rural areas without digital access.
- Using books as hidden communication → printing resistance materials inside normal-looking books.

CHAPTER 18
USING ARTIFICIAL INTELLIGENCE TOOLS

The use of artificial intelligence is a complex and constantly evolving topic. For now, we will leave you with the basics, and encourage you to search on your own for detailed information.

Role of Artificial Intelligence Tools

AI can be leveraged in multiple ways, from increasing the effectiveness of digital activism and cybersecurity to optimizing fundraising and public outreach.

Enhancing Cybersecurity and Anonymity

- AI-Powered encryption:
    - AI can enhance encryption protocols for communication tools, such as messaging apps and email services.
- AI-Driven threat detection:
    - AI can assist in detecting and neutralizing cyber threats in real-time
    - AI can also identify patterns in network traffic that indicate surveillance or targeted attacks by state actors, enabling proactive measures to protect the resistance's operations.

Optimizing Digital Activism and Outreach

- AI-driven social media analysis tools can help resistance groups understand public sentiment, track government propaganda, and identify key areas where support for their cause can be increased.
- Automated content generation:
    - AI can help generate engaging and effective content for social media campaigns, such as slogans, memes, videos, and infographics.
    - AI can even craft persuasive messages tailored to different audiences to spread awareness more effectively.
- Social media bots for amplification:
    - AI can be used to deploy automated social media bots that help amplify messages, counteract regime propaganda, and increase visibility for resistance activities.
- AI for identifying vulnerable groups:
    - AI-powered systems can also be used to analyze demographics and geospatial data to identify areas with large numbers of sympathetic individuals or groups who may be more likely to support a resistance campaign.

Facilitating Anonymous Fundraising

- AI-driven fraud detection systems can help ensure that donations made in cryptocurrencies like Monero are legitimate and secure.
- Optimizing crowdfunding campaigns:
    - AI can analyze donor behavior and predict trends, helping activists optimize their crowdfunding strategies.

- Cryptocurrency transaction analysis:
  - AI can analyze blockchain data to track donations, ensuring transparency and accountability in fundraising, even while maintaining the anonymity of donors.

FACILITATING COMMUNICATION AND COORDINATION

- AI-enhanced secure communication tools:
  - AI can be used to build automated secure communication platforms that analyze and adapt to potential security vulnerabilities.
- Additionally, AI can help detect and filter out misinformation, helping resistance groups stay focused on legitimate, credible sources and messages while filtering out regime-sponsored disinformation campaigns.
- Chatbots for coordination:
  - Resistance groups can use AI-powered chatbots to help coordinate logistical efforts and answer common questions from supporters.
  - For instance, chatbots could guide protesters on how to organize, what legal protections they have, and how to protect their identity online.

MANAGING AND ANALYZING DATA

- Data analytics for strategy:
  - AI-powered analytics can help resistance groups evaluate the success of protests, monitor regime responses, and identify the most effective tactics.
- By processing large amounts of data, AI can identify patterns of repression and make

recommendations on how to minimize exposure to regime countermeasures.
- AI can also process surveillance data, enabling the resistance to develop counter-strategies to evade government tracking and remain undetected.
    - This could involve analyzing patterns in government crackdowns and identifying weaknesses in the regime's control systems.
- Predictive modeling:
    - Predictive analytics powered by AI can help resistance movements understand the likelihood of different outcomes based on various strategies and tactics. For example, AI can predict when protests are most likely to succeed based on historical data or current political climates.

AI in Hacking and Cyberactivism
AI can assist in cyberactivism efforts by

- identifying weak points in government systems,
- automating targeted hacks,
- including deep-fake attacks, and
- disrupting key infrastructures like government websites or surveillance systems.

AI-Driven Disruption
Resistance groups can use AI-driven systems to create targeted disinformation campaigns that expose corruption or human rights abuses. This could involve spreading detailed reports, videos, or articles that undermine the regime's legitimacy without direct confrontation.

AI for Anti-Surveillance
Activists could use AI to mask their digital footprints,

helping them avoid detection by government surveillance systems. This could include AI systems that automatically adjust browsing behavior or encrypt data in ways that make it difficult for the regime to track.

CHAPTER 19
CYBER RESISTANCE METHODS

Hacking and Cyberattacks Basics

Cyberattacks, especially sophisticated ones targeting critical infrastructure or government systems, require a high level of technical expertise. In all cases, such activity is illegal, so proceed with caution.

The information provided here is meant as a framework from which you can begin to research ways to implement strategies and actions.

Skilled hackers or access to underground cyber groups is critical.

However, one small computer alone (like a laptop) could serve as an entry point to escalate an attack.

Full-scale attacks require:

- Network reconnaissance (mapping the target's systems)
- Custom malware development
- Multiple attack vectors (e.g., phishing, software vulnerabilities)
- Coordination from skilled hackers

Here is an overview of basic cyberattack methods and tools used to date:

- Denial-of-Service (DoS) or Distributed Denial-of-Service (DDoS) Attacks:
    - These attacks flood a network or website with traffic, rendering it inaccessible.
    - Resistance could target government websites, law enforcement databases, or communication platforms (such as social media or email servers) to prevent them from functioning properly.

(See below for more detailed information on DDoS attacks)

- Hacking government networks:
    - A more sophisticated approach would involve hacking into government networks to steal, alter, or disrupt crucial information.
    - This could include tampering with communication systems used by government agencies, leaking sensitive data, or spreading disinformation to create confusion.

- Disruption of critical infrastructure or supply chains:
    - Cyberattacks could be used to target critical infrastructure—such as power grids, transportation systems, or financial institutions—leading to widespread disruption.
    - By targeting systems that people rely on every day, a revolutionary movement could increase societal instability.
    - If an attacker compromises one trusted vendor supplying software/hardware to power

companies, for example, they can plant backdoors in many grid systems.

- Propaganda and misinformation:
  - Using cyber tools, resistance members could also distribute propaganda or misinformation on social media platforms, creating confusion, undermining trust in the government, and rallying more people to their cause.
  - Bots or fake accounts could be used to amplify messages that delegitimize government actions or policies.

- Phishing
  - Even a simple laptop can be used to send a spear-phishing email that tricks an employee into installing malware (e.g., BlackEnergy, Industroyer).
  - Once infected, the malware moves laterally within the power company's network.
  - A small device could act as a C2 server to coordinate malware spread inside the target network.

Step-by-Step Guide to Creating a DDoS Attack

DDoS attacks can be illegal and are heavily monitored by authorities, so it's crucial to consider the ethical implications and risks before pursuing such methods.

If you're considering a DDoS attack for activism, ensure that the target is legitimate (e.g., government sites responsible for oppression, not private citizens or non-violent institutions).

- A DDoS attack involves overwhelming a targeted website or server with excessive traffic.
- This traffic comes from a botnet—a network of compromised devices (often computers or IoT devices) that send requests to the target at an overwhelming rate, causing it to crash.

Preparation

- For beginners, there are online platforms that allow you to execute DDoS attacks through a stress-testing service. Many of these may be found by executing searches on Duck Duck Go through the TOR browser.
- While these services are generally used for legal purposes (e.g., testing website resilience), some can be misused for activism.
- Low Orbit Ion Cannon (LOIC): LOIC is an open-source network stress testing tool used to perform DDoS attacks. It's available for free and relatively easy for beginners to use. You can send large amounts of traffic to a target server using this tool.
- High Orbit Ion Cannon (HOIC): an advanced version of LOIC, HOIC is used for stronger DDoS attacks and is more effective at bypassing basic network defenses.
- Botnets: for larger-scale attacks, some activists or hackers create or rent botnets—large networks of compromised devices that can carry out the attack more effectively. However, these tools require advanced knowledge and access to networks of infected devices.

Targets

- Choose a target that is strategically important but also morally justifiable. This could include:
    - Government websites that promote censorship, oppression, or illegal activity.
    - State-run media outlets that spread propaganda.
    - Military or law enforcement websites associated with authoritarian crackdowns.

Start

- LOIC (Low Orbit Ion Cannon): download the tool from a trusted open-source site. Once you have it installed:
    - Open LOIC and enter the IP address or URL of the target website.
    - Choose the attack method (HTTP, UDP, or TCP).
    - Set the request rate. Higher numbers will send more traffic.
    - Begin the attack. LOIC will send requests to the target, overwhelming its server.

Launch and Monitor the Attack

- Once the attack is launched, you will see traffic increase to the target server.
- The server will eventually become overwhelmed and may crash or become slow to respond.
- You can monitor the effectiveness of the attack by checking if the target website becomes inaccessible or slower.

Avoid Detection and Safety Measures

- Use VPNs to mask your IP address and encrypt your internet traffic.
- Use TOR for anonymous browsing and hiding your location.

Cease the Attack and Document Results

- Once you have achieved your goal (such as taking down the site or spreading awareness), stop the attack immediately.
- Document the attack and the results to measure its effectiveness in drawing attention to your cause.

Examples of cyber resistance movements

Anonymous: a decentralized hacktivist collective that emerged in the mid-2000s. Notable actions:

- Attacked Scientology websites in "Project Chanology" (2008).
- Took down Tunisian government websites during Arab Spring (2011).
- Declared cyberwar on Russia after the Ukraine invasion (2022).
- Operation Payback: the group targeted anti-piracy organizations, media outlets, and governments, highlighting concerns over freedom of information and anti-democratic censorship.

WikiLeaks: Founded by Julian Assange, WikiLeaks is an online organization that leaks classified government and corporate documents. Notable leaks:

- Collateral Murder Video (2010) – U.S. military airstrike footage.
- Afghan & Iraq War Logs (2010) – Exposing military operations.
- DNC Emails (2016) – Influencing U.S. political discourse.

Cyber Partisans: a group of Belarusian cyber activists fighting against Alexander Lukashenko's regime. Notable actions:

- Breached Belarusian police records (2021).
- Railway cyberattacks to delay Russian troop movements into Ukraine (2022).

Ukrainian IT Army, a voluntary cyber army formed to defend Ukraine during the Russian invasion. Notable actions:

- Took down Moscow Stock Exchange website (2022).
- Leaked Russian military personnel data.

Hong Kong Protest Cyber Cells, digital activists supporting the 2019 Hong Kong protests against China's control. Notable actions:

- Created AI-generated protest artwork to bypass censorship.
- Used blockchain technology to archive protest materials.

Decentralized Darknet Groups (e.g., Cicada 3301), underground internet groups promoting privacy and free speech. Notable activities:

- steganography & cryptography to share hidden messages,
- encouraging decentralized file-sharing to prevent censorship,
- Tor-based forums to discuss activism in oppressive regimes.

CHAPTER 20
DRONES: AN EVOLVING TOOL FOR ACTIVISM

In the early 2020s, drones have become widespread among amateurs and professionals alike, in use for activities ranging from simple aerial photography to dropping ordnance in the Ukraine/Russia war.

Resistance movements can benefit as well from a variety of uses for drones. Drones can be easily and cheaply acquired.

SURVEILLANCE AND RECONNAISSANCE

- Drones equipped with cameras could be used to monitor government movements, track police or military deployments, and gather intelligence in real-time.
- This could help insurgents plan their next moves, avoid detection, or identify weaknesses in security.

PSYCHOLOGICAL WARFARE

- Drones can be used to create fear, intimidation, or confusion.
- By flying near government buildings or police lines, drones can send a message of defiance and

resistance, demonstrating the insurgents' ability to act from the air.
- This could have a significant psychological impact on both law enforcement and the public.

Delivery of Disruptive Devices and Information

- Some drones can carry payloads, such as electronic jammers.
- Drones could also drop bundles of supplies, leaflets, or other informational materials.

Drone Fleets

The use of drone fleets can have a strong impact on a regime. The key components involved in managing a large fleet of drones include:

- Fleet Management Software:
    - This software is crucial for coordinating the drones and ensuring that they operate safely and efficiently.
    - It allows the operator to monitor and manage multiple drones at once, usually through a central interface.
- Communication Systems:
    - Drones need reliable communication systems, such as a combination of radio frequencies, cellular, or satellite links, to maintain constant communication with the central controller.
    - The communication must be robust enough to handle large numbers of drones.
- Autonomous Flight Capabilities:
    - To manage such a large fleet, drones often need to have a high level of autonomy.

- This includes the ability to make decisions in real-time, navigate around obstacles, and even avoid collisions without direct control from the operator.
- Swarming Technology:
  - Advanced drone fleets often use swarming algorithms, where each drone is aware of its position in relation to the others.
  - This allows for synchronized movements, group tasks (like surveys or mapping), and better coordination.
- Ground Control Stations (GCS):
  - A GCS can be used for fleet management, where the operator controls the drones individually or in groups.
  - In some systems, the operator can manage several drones through automated waypoints or predefined flight plans, with the software handling the details of each drone's movement.
- Network and Power Management:
  - Power management systems are important for ensuring that all drones stay within operational limits, especially for large fleets.
  - Charging stations or battery swap systems could be necessary for extended missions.

This type of fleet management is often used in applications like agriculture, surveillance, search and rescue, or large-scale delivery systems.

The complexity increases with the number of drones, but the technology is certainly available to make it feasible, and costs can be reasonable.

Again, it's important to have a person with technical know-how on your team to carry out such involved activities.

There are many people in the 2020's who would be delighted to participate and contribute their skills to resistance efforts requiring technical skill.

CHAPTER 21
APPLYING SUN TZU'S THE ART OF WAR TO 21ST CENTURY RESISTANCE

The Art of War is a 5th century BC treatise on how to wage war. It emphasizes many subtle points of warfare and has been instrumental to this day in educating military as well as people from all walks of life in achieving their goals.

Here is a brief summary of its main points, how they could be interpreted in a 21st c context, and a longer section on practical applications to certain 2025 USA conditions.

1. STRATEGY AND PLANNING

"*All warfare is based on deception.*"

- Political Application:
    - Messaging and framing of issues should be carefully crafted to appeal to different audiences while disguising true strategic objectives when necessary.
    - For example, a policy proposal might be framed as bipartisan or framed around values the administration already supports to gain traction.

"If you know the enemy and know yourself, you need not fear the result of a hundred battles."

- Political Application:
  - Deep research into key decision-makers, their motivations, and weaknesses can be used to anticipate responses.
  - Understanding both the administration's priorities and your own strengths allows for a more targeted influence strategy.
  - Use online subscription tools like BeenVerified to collect data on individuals and businesses, and Trellis to follow the progression of legal cases.

2. Leadership and Coalition Building
"A leader leads by example, not by force."

- Political Application:
  - Grassroots movements and advocacy groups can gain influence by demonstrating credibility, consistency, and strong leadership.
  - Influencing public opinion can pressure politicians without direct confrontation.

"Treat your men as you would your own beloved sons, and they will follow you into the deepest valley."

- Political Application:
  - Cultivating strong relationships with allies—whether inside government, in the media, or among interest groups—ensures long-term loyalty and support.

3. Adaptability and Flexibility

"Water shapes its course according to the nature of the ground over which it flows."

- Political Application:
    - Policies and messaging should adapt to public sentiment, emerging crises, and political dynamics.
    - A rigid approach will fail in the face of changing political landscapes.

"Opportunities multiply as they are seized."

- Political Application:
    - Timing is critical.
    - Legislative windows, political shifts, or moments of crisis (economic downturns, scandals, foreign conflicts) provide openings to push an agenda when officials are most receptive.

4. Exploiting Weaknesses and Controlling Perception

"Appear weak when you are strong, and strong when you are weak."

- Political Application:
    - Underestimating opposition is a common mistake in politics.
    - A movement or lobbying effort may appear non-threatening while quietly building support, then strike with maximum force at the right moment.

"Engage people with what they expect... while you wait for the extraordinary moment."

- Political Application:
  - Play into existing narratives while preparing a more ambitious shift in policy.
  - Public opinion and media cycles can be manipulated to create surprise advantages.

5. Avoiding Direct Confrontation Unless Necessary

"The supreme art of war is to subdue the enemy without fighting."

- Political Application:
  - Instead of head-on opposition, influence can come from working behind the scenes through bipartisan efforts, economic incentives, or cultural movements that shift policy indirectly.

"When the enemy is relaxed, make them toil. When full, starve them. When settled, make them move."

- Political Application:
  - Keep opponents off balance—introduce new narratives, create distractions, or shift public discourse at crucial moments.

6. Leveraging the Political Terrain

"Know the terrain, and use it to your advantage."

- Political Application:
  - The media landscape, economic conditions, judicial rulings, and public sentiment create the "terrain" of influence. Using them strategically is key.

"Move swiftly where there is no defense. Attack where they least expect."

- Political Application:
  - Identifying overlooked policy areas, bureaucratic loopholes, or weaknesses in political opponents' alliances can allow for unexpected victories.

7. SPEED AND STRATEGIC TIMING
"Speed is the essence of war."

- Political Application:
  - In a fast-moving political environment, acting decisively when an opportunity arises—such as introducing legislation after a major event—can be the difference between success and failure.

"Concerning nonviolence, it is criminal to teach a man not to defend himself when he is the constant victim of brutal attacks." – Malcolm X

PRACTICAL APPLICATION TO TWO 2025 SCENARIOS IN THE USA:

- *Resisting DOGE, and*
- *Advocating for Climate-friendly Policies*

1. RESISTING DOGE

As the Department of Government Efficiency (DOGE) is actively using technology and private-sector technicians to fire government employees and eliminate programs, a strategic response should focus on political, media, legal, and grassroots influence to counteract or redirect their actions.

Below is a Sun Tzu-inspired strategic plan for addressing this issue effectively.

1. *Intelligence & Strategic Positioning (Know Your Enemy & Yourself)*

Gather Information:

- Identify key figures behind DOGE's actions (leadership, contractors, political allies).
- Research their stated justifications (budget cuts, efficiency, ideology) and potential hidden motives (privatization, political maneuvering, weakening government oversight).
- Track how government agencies and employees are being targeted—who is next?

Leverage Weaknesses:

- Look for legal, ethical, or procedural violations in their actions.
- Identify contradictions (e.g., if they claim to promote efficiency but create chaos or cost overruns).
- Expose conflicts of interest (such as ties between DOGE officials and private contractors).

2. *Public Narrative & Perception (The Supreme Art is to Subdue Without Fighting)*

Frame the Issue Effectively:

- Instead of simply opposing DOGE, reshape the public conversation:
    - "This isn't efficiency; it's political purging and privatization."
    - "Slashing USAID harms national security and global influence."

- "Outsourcing government job cuts to tech contractors is reckless and unaccountable."
- Make it a bipartisan issue by showing how it hurts conservative and liberal priorities alike.
  - For example, "USAID cuts harm both international stability (conservatives) and humanitarian efforts (liberals)."
- Engage Key Allies:
  - Government employee unions (AFGE, NTEU) to push back legally and politically.
  - Former program beneficiaries (businesses, veterans, NGOs) who can testify to its importance.
  - National security experts to highlight how programs might support U.S. geopolitical interests.

3. TACTICAL DISRUPTION (MAKE THE ENEMY REACT TO YOU)

Slow Down or Block DOGE's Moves:

- Push for Congressional hearings into the process and legality of these terminations.
- Demand inspector general investigations into contractor roles and potential corruption.
- Lawsuits:
  - Use wrongful termination and whistleblower protections to legally challenge firings.
- Create Political Costs:
  - Publicly expose the human and economic costs (e.g., real stories of fired workers, loss of USAID projects).
- Localize the impact:
  - Show how specific states/districts will suffer from job losses and lost funding.

- Pressure moderate lawmakers who may distance themselves from extreme DOGE actions.

4. ADAPT & REDIRECT (BE LIKE WATER, MOVE WHERE THERE IS NO DEFENSE)

Use Technological Countermeasures:

- If DOGE is using tech experts to cut jobs, use technology to expose and counteract them (leaks, data analysis, transparency efforts).
- Monitor and expose AI-driven decision-making flaws in their job-cutting process.
- Propose an alternative reform plan:
    - Instead of just opposing DOGE, present a competing efficiency strategy that focuses on:
        - Smart reforms that save money without harming workers.
        - Cutting corporate contractor waste instead of essential government jobs.
        - Strengthening program effectiveness rather than eliminating it.

5. SPEED & TIMING (STRIKE WHERE THEY ARE UNPREPARED)

Act Quickly on Public Awareness:

- Organize public campaigns, press releases, and targeted social media campaigns before DOGE's policies are fully implemented.
- Use unexpected supporters:
    - If DOGE expects only Democrats to oppose them, bring in military veterans, religious leaders, or business voices to speak against harmful cuts.
- Exploit internal rifts:

- - Find factions within the administration that are uneasy about DOGE's actions.
- Encourage whistleblowers within the government and contractor network to leak documents or testify.
- Note that DOGE leadership includes businesses that may be harmful to the environment or to communities in which they are operating, such as the large artificial intelligence plant in Memphis, TN, owned by Elon Musk's *Grok Ai*.
  - Capitalize on community resistance to the plant, noting how it uses large quantities of water and electricity to operate.
  - Water and electrical supply are two areas that activists could identify for interruption or for additional publicity.

Sun Tzu teaches that direct confrontation is often the worst strategy. Instead of merely opposing DOGE head-on, the better approach is to:

- Undermine their credibility (highlight contradictions, inefficiencies, and hidden motives).
- Shift public perception (turn the narrative into a bipartisan concern about national stability and responsible governance).
- Use legal, political, and grassroots tools to slow or block their actions.
- Redirect the policy conversation toward better solutions that achieve true government efficiency.

---

2) *Advocating for Climate-friendly Policies*
Strategic Plan for Influencing U.S. Climate Policy (2025)

1. Intelligence & Strategic Positioning (Know Your Enemy & Yourself)

Understand the administration's stance:

- Identify key decision-makers, allies, and blockers within the government (Congress, EPA, DOE, industry lobbyists).
- Track corporate interests (fossil fuels, renewables, tech) that are shaping policy behind the scenes.
- Exploit divisions and weaknesses:
    - Highlight contradictions in policy (e.g., promoting green energy while subsidizing oil and gas).
    - If factions within the administration differ on climate policy, push internal disputes into the public sphere to create pressure.
    - Use data to expose hidden costs of inaction (climate disasters, healthcare burdens, economic losses).

2. Shaping Public Perception (The Supreme Art is to Subdue Without Fighting)

Reframe the climate narrative:

- Move the conversation away from partisan battle lines by tying climate action to:
    - National security (climate-related instability fuels migration, military conflicts, and resource wars).
    - Economic competitiveness (China and the EU are leading in renewables—will the U.S. fall behind?).
    - Job creation (green tech industries create more jobs than fossil fuels).

- Instead of focusing on "climate change," use economic-friendly terms like "energy independence" and "resilient infrastructure." *In fact, this is crucial in 2025 in the USA, as certain phrases such as "climate change" are being physically removed from government web sites.*

Use unconventional messengers:

- Engage groups that conservatives and moderates respect:
    - Military leaders discussing national security risks.
    - Farmers affected by drought and extreme weather.
    - Business leaders investing in clean energy.
    - Religious groups framing environmental responsibility as moral stewardship.

Leverage disruptive events:

- Act immediately after major climate disasters (wildfires, hurricanes, droughts) to push policy urgency.
- Show local economic impacts (cost to homeowners, insurance rates, food prices) to make it personal.

3. Tactical Disruption (Make the Opposition React to You)

Expose hypocrisy & corporate influence:

- Investigate and publicize fossil fuel lobbying efforts that are influencing policy.
- Track where campaign donations are coming from and push transparency measures.

- Highlight inconsistencies (e.g., politicians advocating for "energy security" while blocking renewables).
- Slow down harmful policies, accelerate good ones:
    - Use legal challenges to block rollbacks on environmental regulations.
    - A well-coordinated legal campaign can:
        - Delay or block anti-climate policies through the courts,
        - Create financial and legal risks for polluters and investors,
        - Force the government to enforce existing climate laws,
        - Turn legal victories into political momentum for stronger policies.
    - Push for executive orders when legislative action stalls.
    - Get state governments to adopt stronger climate policies if federal action is weak (California, New York, etc.).

4. STRATEGIC ADAPTATION (BE LIKE WATER, MOVE WHERE THERE IS NO DEFENSE)

Exploit market shifts & economic trends:

- The renewable energy sector is already outpacing fossil fuels in growth—use market momentum to argue that climate action is inevitable.
- Promote climate-friendly investment strategies (ESG funds, clean tech startups) to make green policy seem like a financial necessity.
- Create Win-Win Policy Solutions:
    - Push bipartisan-friendly solutions that appeal to conservatives:

- Carbon capture (instead of outright fossil fuel bans).
- Nuclear energy expansion as a bridge solution.
- Rural solar and wind subsidies for farmers and landowners.

5. Speed & Timing (Strike Where They Are Unprepared)

Introduce policies when opposition is weak:

- Act after election cycles when political risks are lower.
- Capitalize on economic downturns to push green infrastructure as a job-creation solution.
- Use international pressure (if the EU or China takes action, push U.S. competitiveness concerns).

Exploit unexpected allies:

- If opponents expect climate activists to be the only ones pushing, bring in:
    - Tech CEOs framing AI and green energy as the future.
    - Veterans arguing for clean energy independence.
    - Wall Street investors demanding long-term sustainability

CHAPTER 22
MISCHIEF

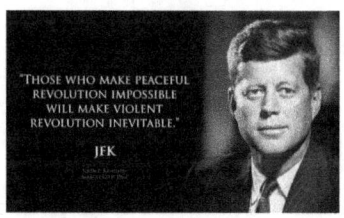

If you are feeling like violence is your only recourse, we would suggest two things:

- (1) leave that to professionals, and
- (2) look it up on the TOR browser

As we said in the very beginning:

*A principled resistance movement attempts to act through ethical guidelines that include not harming other people directly, but it **does not exclude direct actions that may interfere with the functioning** of authoritarian institutions, infrastructure, or "human capital."*

Interfering with the functioning of those items does NOT include physically harming people, so please refer back to our chapter on how to cause human capital disruptions. Also please refer back to the chapter on supply chains.

But to clarify further, here we present some specific examples of human capital, and other institutions and infrastructure that, in the present mid-2025 context in the USA, might be worth investigating.

We are not suggesting harming or threatening people, but we are suggesting that you develop creative ways to let institutions and human capital know that you are aware of their connections to and support for authoritarian powers in the USA.

Human Capital "Supply Chain" Examples:

- Anyone associated with creating Project 2025
- Anyone working with DOGE
- Anyone working for the Trump Administration
- Any Republican member of Congress or the Senate
- Any person or institution that supports any of the above people, such as right wing groups or recently-pardoned J6 individuals
- Anyone on the social media platform X, or other platform, who has a large following and espouses authoritarian viewpoints

Institutions and Infrastructure Examples

- SpaceX, XAi, X, Tesla
- The Trump Organization
  - Hotels, golf courses, etc.
- Businesses owned or controlled by anyone in the above list of human capital
- Suppliers to any of the above businesses

- Businesses that have regular attendance, such as restaurants, of anyone in the above list of human capital

---

If you decide to interrupt the functioning of any of the above, we suggest that you *NOT* do the following:

- Don't send Senators pizza boxes with messages such as "Listen to the people!"
- Don't demonstrate loudly outside the homes of anyone or their families in the human capital list above
- Don't write "Protect the Constitution" with weed-killer spray on a Trump-owned golf course
- Don't send a box of dog excrement to the head of the Department of Homeland Security
- Don't call the parents of DOGE employees to suggest their kids work for America instead of against it
- Don't send steam-punk sunglasses to the head of the FBI
- Don't boycott the businesses of the families of DOGE employees
- Don't send a fleet of remote-controlled toy cars across the White House lawn
- Don't chain yourself around any federal building that has been co-opted by DOGE
- Don't send flowers to pardoned J6 people
- Don't try to cut the electricity or water supply to any of above institutions
- Don't connect with more radical groups such as Antifa, Anonymous, or Redneck Revolt

- Don't seek out bots, viruses, worms, software, or AI tools on sites such as GitHub or dark web sites
- Don't buy books on popular online bookstores published by the US Army on how to build incendiary devices

―――――

In all of the above cases, simple searches on the TOR browser, or by using an identity verification tool such as *"Been Verified,"* will help you to discover what you need.

In addition, on our website, **boomthebook.com,** you will find lists with concrete examples of the above.

BOOM!

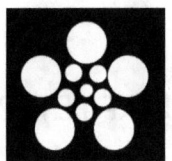

CHAPTER 23
READING LIST

The Wretched of the Earth, Frantz Fanon
Pedagogy of the Oppressed, Paulo Freire
The Conquest of Bread, Peter Kropotkin
The Jungle, Upton Sinclair
A People's History of the United States, Howard Zinn
Discipline and Punish: The Birth of the Prison, Michel Foucault
The Tyranny of the Majority, Lani Guinier
Civil Resistance: What Everyone Needs to Know, Erica Chenoweth
Rules for Radicals, Saul Alinsky
This Is an Uprising: How Nonviolent Revolt Is Shaping the Twenty-First Century, Mark Engler, Paul Engler
The Nonviolence Handbook: A Guide for Practical Action, Michael N. Nagler
Antifa: The Anti-Fascist Handbook, Mark Bray
Rules for Revolutionaries: How Big Organizing Can Change Everything, Zack Exley and Becky Bond
The Art of Invisibility, Kevin Mitnick
The Persuaders: At the Front Lines of the Fight for Hearts, Minds, and Democracy, Anand Giridharadas

The Black Panther Party: Service to the People Programs, Jama Lazerow and Yohuru Williams

The Anarchist Cookbook, William Powell

The Coming Insurrection, The Invisible Committee

How to Blow Up a Pipeline, Andreas Malm

Simple Sabotage Field Manual, US Office of Strategic Services

Authoritarian Regime Survival Guide, anonymous Eastern European Twitter postings from 2017

How To Talk With Anyone About Anything, Harville Hendrix

Beautiful Solutions, and *Beautiful Trouble*, Andrew Boyd, and web project https://beautifultrouble.org/toolbox/, an incredible resource covering ALL of the things one needs

https://canvasopedia.org/publications/, many strong resources for resistance

International Center on Nonviolent Conflict, with its many resources, here https://www.nonviolent-conflict.org/

ABOUT THE AUTHOR

Athena has a long history in teaching, social justice movements, creative writing, and journalism, with experience in Haiti, Afghanistan, the USA, and Europe. Athena has worked for newspapers, as a Buddhist hospital chaplain, in schools, and in various remote and urban environments. Athena's brother was Ares, whose helmet below is the symbol of this imprint.

―――

For more information and to access additional resources pertaining to resistance movements and building democratic states, please visit our website at www.boomthebook.com.

www.ingramcontent.com/pod-product-compliance
Lightning Source LLC
LaVergne TN
LVHW012024060526
838201LV00061B/4438